EVERY DAY IS YOUR BEST DAY

Expect nothing less than wonderful!

Peter Benn

Argosy Media

2 · PETER BENN

"Write it on your heart that every day is the best day in the year."

Ralph Waldo Emerson
Essayist, Lecturer and Poet 1803-1882

14 Proven Wisdoms For Happiness And Abundance You'll Learn From This Book

1. Only you know what you really want
2. Attitude determines your happiness factor
3. Be in tune with the earth's natural rhythms
4. Realize you are connected to everyone and everything
5. Take care of 'Number One' – YOU!
6. Be grateful for everything
7. Stop swimming upstream. Relax and go with the flow
8. Discover your natural-born talent(s) – and grow them
9. Seek to establish perfect health for yourself
10. Carry no unfinished baggage
11. Change is constant – don't fear it
12. Abundance - believe it, feel it and you will receive it
13. Religions often contain overlooked New Earth beliefs
14. You are unique. Celebrate it every day

Copyright Disclaimer

Over my lifetime I have read widely and listened to many on spiritual matters. As a consequence I have absorbed a great many ideas, philosophies and beliefs. Through my own spiritual development I have adapted, grown and lived those that resonated with me the most.

It is my belief that the ideas and philosophies presented in this book are in the public domain, given to us to share and to live by in order to make mankind's earth journey easier and more enlightened.

Should I have accidentally strayed into territory you believe is copyright to you, please contact the publisher so that it can be rectified in future editions.

General Disclaimer

This is not a medical book. All advice and information given is general in nature and non-specific to any individual, couple or group. You are encouraged to seek your own independent medical, psychological and counseling advice. It is not a substitute for your own common sense. The author and publisher shall not be responsible for any person(s) with regard to any loss or damage caused directly or indirectly by the information in this book nor for any damages resulting from the misinterpretation of this work. All details given in this book were current at the time of publication, but are subject to change without notice.

Copyright And Publisher Details

All contents copyright © Peter Benn 2015.

All rights reserved worldwide under the Berne Convention.

Except for brief passages quoted for newspaper, magazine, radio, television or online reviews, no part of this book may be reproduced or transmitted in any form, by any means (electronic, photocopy, recording or otherwise) without the prior written permission of the publisher. Any trademarks, product names or business names are assumed to be the property of the respective owners and are used only for reference. There is no implied endorsement.

Editor: Anthea Wynn

Published by Argosy Media
Postal: PO Box 7615, Melbourne, Victoria 3004 Australia
Email: info@peterbenn.com

ISBN: 978-0-9873337-4-2

Other books by Peter Benn
All titles include paperback and e-book editions.

TALES FROM THE FUR SIDE:
Purrfectly Adorable Cat Stories
Mischief. Mayhem. History. Heroism. Revenge and Reflection. Entertaining and life-affirming stories from the secret lives of cats - as told by the cats themselves. Filled with humor, delightful observation and spiritual insights, this is the ideal gift for everyone who is loved by a cat.

"The stories in this book give you a moral compass to live by." Amazon Review

Mediterranean, European and Baltic CRUISE SHIP EXCURSIONS and SHORE TRIPS:
Exploring 26 Memorable Ports
Get the immediate flavor of 26 ports and cities with this invaluable quick-look planning guide based on the author's actual shore trip experiences. Includes an invaluable checklist of what to take with you to make your shore excursion happy and stress-free.

"This is an extremely practical book." Amazon Review

VERSATILE HUSBAND, The
Answers all the questions a man might ask about same-sex attraction.

"A straightforward practical guide for men in heterosexual relationships who'd like to explore sex with other men. Frank, honest and understanding." Kirkus Reviews

www.peterbenn.com

CONTENTS

14 Proven Wisdoms For Happiness And Abundance You'll Learn From This Book 5
    Copyright Disclaimer, General Disclaimer, Copyright and Publisher Details 6
    Other books by Peter Benn 7
Preface 13
Introduction 21
    My Journey 21
    Releasing The 3D World And Embracing 4D 23
    Your Journey 24
    Three Helpful Definitions 27
THE SPIRITUAL PROMISE 29
    My Transition To The 4th Dimension 29
    From 'Them' To 'Me', From 3D To 4D 31
    Other Signs Of My Transition 36
    Isn't There Something Better Than My Current Lifestyle 39
    Is Transitioning Already Happening Within Your Life 40
3D TREADMILL TO 4D ABUNDANCE 45
    Discovering Why We Are Unhappy 46
    Happiness Factors 46
    Unhappiness Factors 47
    Our Current 3D World - Summary 48
    What Is The Spiritual 4D World 50

- 4D Overview 51
- A Simple Lesson In 4D 53
- I AM – LIVING A JOYOUS EARTH DAY 59
  - My Day Begins With … 64
  - The Law Of Attraction 65
  - Throughout My Day… 69
  - End Of The Day Gratitude Prayers 83
- RELIGIONS AND CELEBRATIONS 87
  - Learning From Religions 87
  - New Age Philosophy And Christianity 92
  - Learning From Christian Celebrations 94
- RESOLVING SOME BIG QUESTIONS 103
  - Honesty 105
  - Remaining Positive 107
  - Keeping Your Mouth Shut 109
  - Love Another As You Would Be Loved 110
  - Why Is A Particular Someone In My Life 112
  - The Negative Influence 113
  - Change Is Constant – Don't Fear It 115
  - Our Place In The Universe 117
- BE THE PERSON YOU WANT TO BE 121
  - Unfinished Business 122
  - Address Your Addictions And Phobias 125
  - Say Goodbye To Self-Sacrifice 126
  - Stop Swimming Up-Stream 128
  - Seek, Discover And Embrace Your Talents 130
  - Make Your World A Fairer And Spiritual One 133
  - Understand Anger 134

CREATING MATERIAL ABUNDANCE 137
Thought Creates And Attracts Abundance 137
Money 139
Say 'Yes' To Maintain The Flow Of Abundance 141
If In Doubt, Test Yourself 145
More About Practicing Manifestations 147
You *Are* A Creator 151
The Keys To A Better Life 153

ENCOURAGING GOOD HEALTH 157
Exercise 157
Eating Pure, Natural Foods 159
Eat Something That You Have Grown 161
Embrace Source 163
Our Second Brain 166
Embrace Holistic and Complementary Health Therapies 166
Walk With Nature 168
Bless Your Home With Fragrance 169
Use Eco-Friendly Products 172

LIVING THE NEW EARTH PHILOSOPHY 175
Living A Purer, Happier And More Harmonious Life 175
Share Your Life With A Pet 176
Find Good In Everything 178
Bring Stillness In To Your Life 179
Thank Your Unseen Support Staff 182
Let Your Inner Child Have Fun 183
Spontaneous Dancing 184
Living With The Abundance Of Life 185
Admire The Delicate Petals Of A Flower 187

Frequently Give Thanks 188
Celebrate Every Day 189
Adjust Your Self-Image 190
Just Be Yourself 193
Positive Mental Attitude 194
Be Outgoing And Friendly 195
Enjoy Your Abundance 197
Continue Using, Don't Unnecessarily Replace 198
Laugh At Yourself 201
Smile 201
Share Kindness 202
YOU ARE… 205
No One Else Sees The World Like You Do 205
Live For Today 206
Your Legacy 207
Your Every Day Reality Mirrors Who You Really Are .. 209
I Am Unique. You Are Unique 210

Preface

"Set your sights high, the higher the better. Expect the most wonderful things to happen, not in the future but right now. Realize that nothing is too good. Allow absolutely nothing to hamper you or hold you up in any way."

- Eileen Caddy
Author and Co-Founder Findhorn Foundation 1917-2006

Whatever your current circumstances, *you* can begin now to transform your life and start enjoying the benefits you most want to have.

Welcome to the keys to your future!

Am I right in assuming that your life right now isn't as easy as you imagine it should be?

Your love life (if there is any) is dismal. You're always short of money. You have wonderful dreams that lie dormant and remain out of reach. You're short on time, long on stress. You're exhausted with nothing much to show for it. Increasingly you live in a cyber world without physical human interaction. You're unhappy and you don't know how to turn that around. You're spiritually restless about all sorts of issues.

If any of these resonate in your life, then it's time to unplug for a few hours and listen to your elders and what they've got to say.

Remember those childhood times when your parents or grandparents seemed to always be giving you advice about this or about that. Your teachers were no better. And the minister of your church thundered it out from the pulpit every week. It seemed like a never-ending stream of do-this, do-that, don't touch that, walk this line, share that, burn in Hell for that.

After a time, you grew older and discovered an ability to turn off to such platitudes and advice. You grew into an independent young person with your own thoughts and ways of doing things. "What did those oldies know about real life anyway? I'll do it my way!"

Now you realize that as hard as you have tried, life has not worked out quite as well as you had hoped. So why have you forgotten all of those teachings implanted in you by all of those adults during your childhood?

I suggest that you haven't forgotten them at all – they are just buried deep within you patiently waiting to be rediscovered.

As a child you soaked up everything that was said or done around you. You learned from hearing, seeing, observing, experiencing. You started to make judgments for yourself based on what you knew about life. As is usual with teens, perhaps you revolted against the restraints your parents set for you, their standards, their seeming conservatism, their lack of understanding about how you needed to live a better, more interesting life than they were capable of.

Adult life meant freedom to be yourself – to live, love, enjoy, build, learn and experience everything this wonderful world has to offer.

So why hasn't it worked out for the better? Is it that you are living someone else's ideal life? Could that be the 'approved' career and lifestyle choice your parents made for you in order to have their own dreams fulfilled through you? Deep inside your own dreams still flicker alive from time to time and this adds to your frustration and unhappiness.

Have you removed your lifestyle too far from a connection to the natural rhythms of the earth? When was the last time you ate a fresh vegetable or herb from your own garden and luxuriated in the exquisite taste of freshly picked food? Or hiked in the forest, paddled in the ocean or lazily watched clouds pass on a warm summers afternoon.

And what of a soul-mate and other interesting people in your life? Why are you deflecting such people from sharing good times with you? And why are others using you for their own ends?

Abundance – you can see this all around you, but why does it bypass your door and deliver elsewhere? I'm going to show you that simply by changing a negative approach to life to a positive one you can get immediate results.

This book sets out to explore many of the issues that might have influenced your adult decisions and then show how to rediscover the life skills given to you in childhood. But more than that, this is a guide to connect you to the *spiritual* aspects of your life journey.

Life skills and spirituality are not independent of one another; they are totally entwined. Embrace the spiritual aspects and your life will immediately change for the better. Foster good health and a happy, positive outlook and you may even live longer.

Change comes about when you start the simple process of *wanting* to feel better about yourself, of *wanting* to leave behind those aspects of your life that are unfulfilling, of *wanting* the material as well as spiritual comforts of life - and then taking the *action* to create it and bring it in to your life.

Beginning from a standing start it takes a lot of energy to overcome that inertia. But like that famous quote says, the first step is the most important action you can take in order to move closer towards your destination. And then take another. And another.

As for your dreams, once you get that little tingle of excitement that says *your* dream *may* be possible you won't be able to shake it. It's like a seed having reached fertile ground, and is determined it will stay there until the roots sprout and take hold in the soil.

Once that is achieved then no storm, no matter how powerful, will pull it from the earth. Once your dream takes root, you too will feel invincible. Now is the time to release that inherent energy that resides within you.

I am also going to share with you the fact that you are a perfect soul. That as a fragment of Source (or God, as you may know it) you are not only connected to everyone and everything, you already have the perfection and pure love of that energy Source.

Knowing that you *are* Source gives your day guidance, a solid grounding, a place that is fantastic to dwell in. Your positive attitude to the world and its inhabitants shines forth to others and is a beacon of possibility for them to consider. Your day runs smoothly, happily and with contentment. Wealth and abundance no longer pass your door – they enter and entwine into your life. Your health begins to glow and you have more energy. There's relief from the burdens you've carried on your shoulders. You sleep easily and soundly. Fears dissipate. Relationships are seen in their clarity and you instinctively know if changes are required. Others see you as dynamic, centered and attractive so they want to share meaningful time with you. You begin to search for activities and like-minded people in order to grow your life. You no longer feel second-rate, insecure or fragile.

You're now part of the dynamic life-stream. You've teamed up and ride with the greatest power in the universe. Feel it, savor it, encourage it, live it! Make every day your best day, for this is *your* own journey to happiness and success!

During my sixty plus years, I have lived a divergent lifestyle that has ranged from student poverty to comfortable abundance, from teenage nerd to spiritual seeker, from rural childhood to suburbanite, from fatherhood to free soul. And I do indeed live the life I write about.

Somewhere within my words you will find the keys to what *you* are looking for to make the positive changes in *your* life. You have not 'accidentally' chosen this book to read. It has reached your hands because you have already put out a plea to the universe for help. You know full well that it is time for the person you see in the mirror to change to become the person you want to be.

Because I am introducing to you a new belief system your thoughts may be challenged. You may consider some ideas fanciful. Other ideas will touch deep within you to some dormant place of long forgotten wisdom. There will be times when you will instinctively 'know' that what is written is truth and it's exactly what you know you need. That's a 'wow' moment you'll forever be thankful for.

As you read this and other spiritually based books, your philosophical backpack will fill with useful beliefs. Together they will give you all the elements of *your* own personalized plan for happiness and abundance. Maybe it will be *"Debbie's Every Day Live-Like-A-King Happiness Plan"* or *"Jim's Confidence Plan For The Building Of My Business Dream"*. Personalize your plans by giving them a name – and then begin to live them with all the gusto and happiness their name implies.

The writing here comes directly from *my* heart and *my* experience. I know that they are universal truths that my unseen guides, teachers and angels have assisted me in writing.

May my words and *your actions* combine to introduce you into a new, happy, confidant, loving, and grateful lifestyle with wonderful benefits financially, materially and spiritually. You deserve nothing less. It's your birthright! Enjoy the journey.

> *"To become what we are capable of becoming is the only end in life."*
>
> – Robert Louis Stevenson
> Scottish Novelist 1850-1894

Introduction

My Journey

I have been alive on the earth-plane over 60 years – but only recently have I begun to live!

I feel absolute joy and happiness, I feel connected to nature and mankind, I attract abundance and I've found my own inner peace.

Why has it taken me so long to learn and appreciate these things? Where was that elusive one-stop spiritual handbook I needed to guide me?

Others around me seemed to lead financially abundant lives, they traveled a lot, lived in large modern houses with all the trappings, had well-paid and interesting jobs and overall led a charmed existence.

However, I also observed a darker side of these abundant lives. Wealth was often coupled with tragedy, family breakdown, ill health, disaster and loss, which in turn brought anger, fear, unhappiness and worry.

Surely there must be a compromise position, a happy medium, where enough money and possessions do not attract the darker forces of retribution, where karma is not out of balance.

Wherever I looked, I couldn't find it.

My discontent began in my teen years where I was an outsider from my school's social structure. My negative self-image and low self-esteem therefore became part of my life-skills.

As an adult, I yearned for knowledge of things 'spiritual' in the broadest sense. So I read widely on spiritual and New Age philosophies. I attended classes, churches, seminars and practitioners. I embraced much of what I learnt or had been stimulated by and the best of these yielded me a lifetime of spiritual value. Sometimes the enthusiasm for a particular philosophy would quickly wane so the search would continue.

Over the last couple of decades I've enjoyed being my own self. I enjoyed freedoms of employment, thought and action. I worked from home thus avoiding the insane daily commute. Being self-employed meant that I had to be self-reliant. And of vital importance, I built a period for spiritual nourishment into every day.

Finally, around the age of sixty, I realized that I had actually enjoyed an emotionally rich, textured life and I was already living in peace, love and harmony. I was healthy, my faculties were all intact and giving me pleasure. I was financially able to travel to see this world for myself. I saw the earth as a place of infinite beauty and wonder. I had joy filling my heart and a contentment that I suspect comes with age. Thus I began to reflect on my journey so far.

Releasing The 3D World And Embracing 4D

By 2012, the last days of the 26,000-year Mayan calendar cycle, I knew there would be spiritual and vibrational changes to our world and way of life. I recognized that when one era of mankind closes and the portals to a new age open, it's a stunningly wonderful and unique time to be alive.

The 3D world is the way that we as humanity have been living - at best it is a functional, factional, ego driven, masculine managed, feudal-style structured society. It's fuelled by greed and money, minority rule, anger, ego, control, lust and religious intolerance – and it is unsustainable.

4D reveals that we are connected to every one and every thing in the entire universe. Any abundance we desire already exists and all we have to do is attract it. Hurt your fellow human and you injure yourself. No recriminating karma. By living totally as the energy source, the God Source of the universe, expect peaceful, happy, abundant and joyous days. It is life lived through the loving heart and not the ego.

It wasn't long before the knowledge of the Light Workers, those enlightened teachers of wisdom who are on earth to bring us this New Age good news, found me.

By understanding that our past has been a 3D treadmill and our future is 4D abundance and harmony, all has fallen in to place for me. I realized that my whole life has been preparing for this new era. I have in fact been living much of 4D without knowing it.

Your Journey

And now I invite you to discover 4D living for yourself.

This book gives you ideas and choices. It encourages you to prepare your own action plan by selecting those practices that resonate most strongly with you, building them in to your life – and then being prepared to be amazed.

You can expect déjà vu from re-visiting your childhood religious teachings or from the life-skills your parents drilled in to you. You might receive instant emotional prods where you instinctively know a truth and you might also embrace amazing new thoughts and ways of seeing and thinking.

At the end of each chapter there is a simple action plan deriving from what was discussed. Use these pointers to help reinforce your new ways of thinking, but particularly use them to instigate action, for without action nothing will change.

These words are all cornerstones to living a successful 4D life. Embrace them and they will become your very thinking, your very actions, every hour and minute of every day. They become as important to you as breathing, as your heartbeat, as the pulse of life itself.

After reading this book and putting your selected action plan together, my prayer is that you will also have re-connected with your loving heart. It's the grandest, warmest, most fantastic place you will ever reside.

Open your eyes and your heart, and together let's explore this heavenly new world of possibility. Delve in to my world and see the world through my eyes – and more importantly – through my heart.

The world is a beautiful, joyous, peaceful and stunningly intricate place to be. There's fun, interest, excitement, calmness. It's whatever you want it to be.

But one thing – it's *never* dull.

Three Helpful Definitions

Love

Love is the energy that fuels my life, my very being. It gives me connection to everything in the universe. It raises my vibration levels. It is my greatest gift that I can share. It gives me a sense of peace, place and purpose. It releases me from the 3D man-made world of control over, and judgment of others. Love is limitless. You know that within your own soul that you are pure love and no matter how much you share that with others your capacity to be filled with love is not reduced.

Unconditional Love

It's love with no conditions, boundaries, limits, pre-conceived notions, if, buts or may be. It is freely given without any thought or expectation of receiving anything in return. Unconditional love is the life energy that sustains us all.

Source

I use the word Source as the powerhouse at the centre of the universe from which everything derives. You might use God, Father, Energy, Supreme Being, Jehovah, Elohim, Yahweh or one of many other names. If you are reading this as a non-believer in New Age/New Earth philosophies then the scientific approach through Quantum Theory could be the right name for you.

CHAPTER ONE

THE SPIRITUAL PROMISE

"We are all visitors to this time, this place. We are just passing through. Our purpose here is to observe, to learn, to grow, to love... and then we return Home."

- Indigenous Australian Aboriginal Proverb

My Transition To The 4th Dimension

More than a decade ago I met and spent quality time with a man trained in counseling. He has recently passed to higher life and of late, I have been reflecting on his influence on me and upon the way I look at my life as a subsequence.

For he introduced me - to me!

I see now that my spiritual move from the old 3rd to the new 4th Dimension began at that time. Often it takes hindsight for us to appreciate the positive values of a person who joined us on our path sometime earlier. This meeting might only be a fleeting one of a few minutes, or it could be a shared friendship over many years. Through osmosis, we absorb their energy, their ideas and their vibrations – for good or for bad.

In my case, a seed was planted in the fertile soil of my heart. It grew over the next decade until I was ready to embrace the New Earth energies when they arrived during 2012 and 2013. These extraordinary energies have showered down from the cosmos to enable the human spiritual journey to progress at a much more rapid pace than in any other previous time span.

Like the seedling, I knew not what was happening to me nor had control over it. I was alive, growing, being enriched by my environment, peacefully existing. My spiritual DNA - those encoded spiritual instructions at the core of my being - were organically growing me without me having to think about it.

When the new energies arrived they acted like the Sun. I was warmed, I absorbed the energies, growth happened rapidly, I budded, I blossomed, I was truly alive and soon was living a peaceful and abundant existence.

Let me now retrace some of these steps in more detail as it is possible that they could resonate to help you realize your abundant potential as a joyous and comforted 4th Dimension spiritual person.

From 'Them' To 'Me', From 3D To 4D

My journey to the new spiritual philosophy began with an internal personal shift from 'them' to 'me'.

Up to that point I had been living my life following the creed that I should be of unswerving assistance to everyone I knew. Not a bad philosophy I thought, but it meant that I was like a cork being tossed around on a wild sea with no control over what, who, when or where. I was at everyone else's disposal and because I rarely said no to anyone's request, that meant I was heading for exhaustion.

My own perception of me, or more precisely, what I *thought* was the perceived image that I carried within me that I had to live up to, was the real issue. Indeed I was living a fantasy life that totally reflected what I thought *others* expected of me.

Something had to be done to take control of my life.

My friend did just that – by insisting that I focus on me – what *I* wanted, what bought *me* comfort and pleasure, what helped grow *me* spiritually, doing only what made *me* happy.

As this was such a diametrically opposed view to the life I was living I protested that it was not possible as I'd lose all my friends, my family would hate me, my business clients would abandon me, I'd be viewed as a selfish individual – none of the things I felt I could afford to have disappear from my life.

Yes, it was my ego talking and it was in full protection mode. All of my social conditioning was rebelling, reminding me that I would be pitifully alone and rejected if I dared follow this new 'me' philosophy.

My friend was adamant, and because I wanted (and needed) the change in my life, he became my guiding star, a conscience buddy sitting on my shoulder. That is, whenever I spoke about "having to do so and so for so and so" he'd stop me and ask why do I want to do that, what's in it for me, wouldn't you rather be using that time to do something that grows you?

He was so constant and decisive in his actions that what began as a stand-over tactic of me having to say no to my requester soon moved to become a new pattern of behavior for me. I quickly learned to start analyzing not only my behavior but also that of those who were wanting from me. It didn't take long before I had one of those "eureka" or "wow" moments where in a split second there is crystal clarity.

From that moment on it was the new me in the saddle. I was in charge of me. I was capable of saying "sorry, but I can't help today." Others were no longer controlling me for their advancement or convenience. I was no longer at their disposal. I no longer had to justify my way of life.

I was excited to reallocate my time to doing something that was of personal or spiritual importance to me.

Certainly a few people who could no longer see me as being useful to them fell by the wayside. Others were very surprised at the new me, but took the changes in their stride.

So what was now different?

Firstly, there was a new self-respect for myself as an individual. Until you've experienced this it is difficult to adequately describe the emotion.

Because you are now making a bold statement about the inner you to the outside world in everything that you do and say, it both emerges from you as well as reflects back to you. There is an inner confidence that says, "I'm me, here I am, take me or leave me. I'm happily content living my own life in a peaceful, abundant and spiritual manner."

And you know what? People are very attracted to that image.

It's my belief that when I began concentrating on my individual spiritual journey that I connected to Source in a knowing way. My birthing from Source was always there, and I had always latently been connected, but now I mentally acknowledged this connection.

Source to me is the God-force, the pure love and energy that is and that drives every molecule in the universe. Without my recognizing of it, I could have been born, lived and died, just like the majority of life, without ever having had the slightest knowledge of my part in the Cycle of Life.

But as a soul having an earthly journey I am now very aware of my spiritual existence here. I know that I am made up of millions of molecules and atoms, and possess a human shape. I know too that because of the energy in the molecules and atoms, that I am total energy. As the soul inhabiting this human body I have total control over it. The more I knowingly connect with Source and the energy of love, then the more my body glows with enthusiasm, higher vibrations and good health.

It is this energy mass that attracts like-minds to you. It attracts your abundance, it attracts love and peace and harmony. It attracts those who want to be with you. Energy and harmonious vibrations are what set you apart from other humans. Humans are intrinsically attracted to energy whether that be a human smile, a super-fit dedicated sports-person, a lecturer who sparkles with inner emotion and commitment, a music performance piece or a gentle human being who glows with good health and a twinkle in the eye.

Secondly, I was now open to new experiences, new people and new spiritual development.

With my new inner confidence I was happily content with my onward journey. And what came to me was not only knowledge via books, articles, internet explorations, etc, but warm-hearted and loving people. They could see who I was, what I stood for, how I conducted my life – and yet they still wanted to share with me.

That lingering doubt about my perceived inadequacies still occasionally haunts me even after a decade of forward journeying. Therefore be prepared that a lifetime of insecurity takes a very long time to remove completely.

Love came to me and I happily set up house with a new partner, a relationship that continues to this day.

I journeyed through this last decade with old friends and many new ones.

Having withdrawn from it over many years I returned to investigating spirituality in its many forms. New friends encouraged me in this and together we forged personal links and knowledge that has been of benefit to each other in a shared way.

I learned to live each day gracefully, peacefully, with love and with gratitude.

Thirdly – seven years into this decade of growth there seemed to be something missing from my life – like satisfaction in my employment and a nagging something in the head that suggested the importance of sharing my knowledge, making the world a better place and leaving a legacy for future generations. How, where and why not, still needed answers.

Other Signs Of My Transition

Instinctively I knew that I needed to change direction in my life if I wanted to succeed in following my heart to undertake the teaching I have always suspected I was capable of but never allowed myself to explore.

I was now at the beginning of the final third of my life here on earth, so it had to be now or never. My everyday work environment was in decline and that gave me more time to pursue alternatives. There were two big dreams that have been part of me all my adult life – (1) to make documentary films, and (b) to write books and articles.

It was coming close to the end of the calendar year, so a good time to say that I'd devote at least the next twelve months to one of them and see what happens.

I'd spent more than three years researching, documenting and interviewing a close-to-my heart story that would, as a completed program screen to the peak Sunday night television audience. It was of important cultural and historical significance, it was highly entertaining, most of the storytellers who could share the story in their own words were still alive and from what I would learn technically by its production it would open up a whole new world of future documentaries that I could make (especially based on spiritual subjects). I was also relatively inexperienced in production, so to obtain funding I would have to find an experienced producer, who, despite much searching, had not to that point revealed him/herself to me.

Separately, I've been told throughout my entire life that I have a skill for writing, for seeing the world a little differently, seeing it more humanely and with an ability to walk in the shoes of someone else.

"Why aren't you writing all this down" was a common statement – and I instinctively knew that I should be.

About this time I heard the name Light Worker for the first time. Instinctively I knew that it also belonged to me and that I was here to share in the worldwide illumination of the human spirit.

As humanity, we need to understand and practice love and harmony, obtain knowledge of the fragility and interconnectedness of all life, replace the masculine strength ideal with the feminine and maternal, and to live in peace and higher vibration leaving war and aggression to dissolve into nothingness.

Somewhere deep within me a chink opened that let out the previously hidden knowledge that this was my key to why I live this earth life. Suddenly, I realized that I was 'Home'.

As all this knowledge was inside me waiting to be shared with others, it was not difficult to choose the year of writing. The choice did actually surprise most of my friends who were unaware of the inner spiritual me, that hidden area where those issues were already very gestated.

With the end of the last Mayan Calendar in 2012 whatever the beliefs of others, mine focused on the fact that to be alive at such a significant moment in earth time would offer me deeper and more meaningful paths of existence. Connecting to the beginnings of this new spiritual era, my life now seemed filled with amazing possibilities.

Isn't There Something Better Than My Current Lifestyle

You know there is, but on a global scale you are overwhelmed by your perception of the size of the problem. As a result you have fears, anxieties, depression. You ask yourself how, as collective humanity, we got this way and why does there seem to be nothing we can do about it.

What can one person in over seven billion do to make the necessary changes?

Research by David R. Hawkins estimates that as a single active spiritually aware person we counteract the negative consciousness of at least 800,000 persons. And as we actively pursue and practice spirituality the higher that figure becomes.

What you are hearing within you is a-call-to-spiritual-arms. By making a positive start to changing your own life, in due course your refreshed spiritual life will be an example to others. By putting in to effect the actions that you identify with, then the flow of energy, that life-stream, will begin flowing within and through you.

You *can* and *will* make a difference to both yourself and the planet.

But heed the caution:

> *Don't only be a collector of knowledge,*
> *be a practitioner of action!*

As you learn how to move from your fearful, anxiety driven current 3D world towards the 4D one, this new knowledge will give you a warm, fuzzy, comfortable feeling for a time – but without *action* nothing will happen to *change* your circumstances.

It's *action* through unconditional love, gratitude and desire that will turn your life around, for these are the fundamentals of your new sustainable and loving 4D world.

If you want to feel the life forces in you, feel the benefits of a healthy body, live in physical abundance, assist the earth in her recovery, enjoy the inner calm that has eluded you for so long – then *action* and not just knowledge, is what is required.

Any change for the better is entirely up to you. I believe that you can do it - and therefore I give you my deepest love and admiration in your quest.

Is Transitioning Already Happening Within Your Life

Perhaps you have already noticed some of these first signs of your 4D affinity…

- ✓ Good things are starting to materialize in your life – even from just a passing thought

- ✓ Concern for our Earth. You've become pro-active in recycling, begun growing some of your own food, you have a more active interest in global environmental organizations

- ✓ Concern for injustice – newspapers and the media constantly barrage you with social injustice stories and you have had enough. It's time to turn the tide towards equal human rights for all humanity

- ✓ Feeling for others in emotional crises such as death and injury. You strongly empathize with your fellow humans who are doing life very hard. You especially feel a closeness to those enduring tragedy and pain

- ✓ Alert to the feelings of others. Instinctively you know that you can offer wisdom, empathy and an understanding heart to an individual in need even if they have not spoken of their circumstances

- ✓ No desire to win anymore or to beat someone else. You're tired of the 'rat race', the one-upmanship, of the treadmill feeling. You have looked at your life and decided that at last you are happy to progress with what you have at hand – your body as it is, the comforts of your home as you now have them and the peace of mind that comes with contentment of the now

- ✓ You want to give back rather than take. You'd like to volunteer a few hours to a worthy cause, teach a younger person a particular skill, be pro-active in making change where you can uniquely best achieve it

- ✓ You're observing positive and harmonious changes in other parts of the world – and that encourages you. You can see love and humanity and peaceful ways starting to appear. Against all the old conservatism, negativity and against all the odds, the world *is* changing and you want to encourage that along

- ✓ You observe that in some regions there is a reversion to very conservative and controlling political activity. You instinctively know that such events are the final anachronistic death throws of strong-arm regimes where they are having their last moment in the sun before the new order of love and harmony sweeps through. Because you now know that all of humanity, wherever they reside, are your brothers and sisters you now feel a new kinship, affinity and confidence within you

- ✓ You're discontented with your home/work environment. You are finding it harder to balance the need to put food on the table and provide a comfortable home environment with the wasted earth resources you are helping to deplete

- ✓ There's that 'round peg in a square hole' feeling where you are not being true to your inner self. Would outdoor work be more fulfilling that sitting behind a desk pushing paper or computer keys?

- ✓ You're more aware of community concern over issues of waste, political expediency, inequality of humanity, environmental damage, etc and you want to join with other like-minded people to stop or inhibit the power of the world's controllers

If any of these thoughts and observations echo those of yours, then you are being presented with an opportunity to change. Instinct is telling you that right now things are not right and something has to be done to improve your life.

It's time to begin making the changes – and these will begin *within* you.

> "The secret of change is to focus all of your energy, not on fighting the old, but on building the new."
>
> - Socrates
> Greek Philosopher 469–399BC

☐☐☐☐☐

♥ *My Action Plan*

- ☐ I realize that I am already in transition from the 3D world to the New Earth 4D one

- ☐ I am no longer overwhelmed by world issues

- ☐ I am ready and willing to change my thoughts, my attitudes and my desires. I'm empowered as a "practitioner of action!"

    Tell me more …

CHAPTER TWO

3D TREADMILL TO 4D ABUNDANCE

"We tend to forget that happiness doesn't come as a result of getting something we don't have, but rather of recognizing and appreciating what we do have."

- Fredrick Koenig
Inventor 1774-1833

This has been my journey from the third to the fourth dimension (3D to 4D). I share this with you to assure you that there is a happier way, a more loving way of living.

With your active embracing of 4D you'll see the world differently, more compassionately and with a confidence and surety that you instinctively know has been missing from your everyday world of the third dimension.

Take from my experiences any or everything that intrinsically feels right to embrace.

Discovering Why We Are Unhappy

You don't need to be 'spiritual', 'alternative', 'hippie', 'environmental warrior' or 'politically active', nor identify with any other labels in order to be seeking a new and sustainable belief system. Every person is entitled to manifest whatever he or she instinctively knows that they need in their life.

"I just want to be happy!" is a cry that is commonplace in these current troubled times. As are "I'm always short of money", "why does life have to always be so hard" and "she's always lucky and wins everything".

If any of these resonate then we can replace your envy, jealousy or lack of abundance with happiness, contentment and comforts – and it won't cost anything more than your time and your focused attention.

Happiness Factors

- Happy people really annoy those who are unhappy and discontented. That says to me that our natural state should always be happy and joyful as it's the one we all strive to be in

- We use fewer muscles to smile than to frown – it's effortless. Whereas to frown or express anger we have to work at it and make a decision to look the unhappy way we do

- Perennially happy people seem to have more friends, less illness, look more attractive and when you are with them, time passes so much more quickly. We observe and absorb that happiness, seemingly getting our own pleasure from the vibrations they give out

Unhappiness Factors

- Jealousy leads the unhappy person to believe that the other's happiness was probably achieved at their expense

- The image of the happy person is also a niggling reminder to the unhappy person of what their life might be "if only…."

- Grumpy, discontented people constantly complain, but still allow themselves to wallow in unhappiness. It's as if there is a security in having something to complain about. While that status quo remains, then unsettling change is avoided

- There can also be envy when a happy person walks in to the room – "if only she knew the burdens and problems I have to put up with she wouldn't be walking around with that self-centered smile on her face. Obviously she doesn't have kids, or obsessive in-laws or a demanding boss or money troubles or …"

- An unhappy person sends out a very negative message about their own life – constantly reiterating a message of envy, disgruntlement, scarcity and lack of love. They are unable to quieten their inner babble in order to listen, observe or absorb. Negativity and jealousy have become their guiding stars.

Does any of this mirror your life?

It did for me, for years and years - until I had my sea-change resulting in a change of attitude and a new perspective on life.

If you're seeking happiness, material abundance, joy, calmness, security or harmony then it's time to begin to change your thoughts. This will cost you nothing but a little of your thinking time every day.

In my eyes, that's not only the bargain of the century but of all time.

Our Current 3D World - Summary

Third Dimension (3D) thinking, living and acting includes:

- ✓ Being in pursuit of excessive material abundance
- ✓ Being money obsessed

- ✓ Being self-centered and always believing you are right about everything, backed up by an attitude of no tolerance toward change, alternative lifestyles, social or religious deviation

- ✓ Thinking and acting only with your head and ego

- ✓ Having lack of time for others

- ✓ Having lack of thought for others

- ✓ Having a belief in personal inadequacy regarding your place in the world, how others treat you, and what you can or can't achieve

- ✓ Believing in karma payback through bad health, lack of money, poverty, etc all because of your negative emotions and beliefs

- ✓ Your ego constantly stepping in to re-assure you not to even try to better yourself; you're unworthy

- ✓ Carrying an attitude that life was meant to be difficult for the masses but indulgent and easy for a few. You are therefore envious and more than a bit angry

- ✓ A need to be more of a know-all or superior to your friends and neighbors

- ✓ An awareness of the negativity and envy that surrounds financial riches and the jealousy of others, especially within a family

- ✓ A lottery mentality where financial riches and quality of life are *wished* for without a need to work for them

- ✓ A carefree, careless attitude towards the earth's resources

- ✓ Life feeling like being on a treadmill where you have no control over change for your betterment

- ✓ Anything else that you feel, or instinctively know, that needs changing. For it is those things that tell us what we need to replace or modify in order to live a more humane and spiritual way.

So what would be different in a 4D world?

What Is The Spiritual 4D World

It is the Cycle of Life as lived through your heart rather than as at present, through your ego. It's how we integrate all aspects of mind, body and soul with our earthly existence between birth and death.

4D Overview

The 4th Dimension is the reality of dwelling in a world of total health, love, light, happiness, abundance and peaceful calm.

- ✓ In the sense of time, everything is in the now. Now is where we live - this very moment

- ✓ You recognize that you are born from Source (or whatever you already believe that central energy/God source to be), that you therefore *are* Source, and that you *are* perfect

- ✓ That you as energy are connected to every other particle in the entire universe and in all dimensions, whether these particles of energy be human, animal, plant or other static matter – and that when you as matter decompose, you will return to Source to be part of future physical forms

- ✓ You love your enemies just as much as loving your family. All humans are connected to you and therefore interdependent on one another

- ✓ You see the world through your heart not through your head or your conscious brain. Ego and its insidious destructive effects are banished

- ✓ Karma has been removed from your life – revenge, retribution to others, hurt – these are now gone from your lexicon

- ✓ A new feeling of confidence because you see yourself as no longer overwhelmed by being a mere droplet in a vast ocean of humanity

- ✓ Everything you desire for an earth-plane life already exists – money, happiness and perfect health. All you need to do is to learn to perform a manifestation request from the heart in order to bring it to you

- ✓ Your own particular world is based on inner peace. You have inner calm, you're more tranquil, less aggressive and you sleep easier and more soundly. The speed of life slows down because you've deleted the aggressive material desires from your life

- ✓ Each day you wake to a peaceful heart and the glorious, joyful possibilities the new day has to offer

- ✓ 3D fear is replaced with a seeking of balance in everything you do

- ✓ Decisions are now conscious choices of the heart

- ✓ Through your affirmations, abundance, harmony and joy constantly appear in your life

- ✓ You allow the free flow of the life-stream to happen and no longer fight against its current

- ✓ You live in a spiritual place where the world's negative events no longer interest or affect you

- ✓ You feel as one with nature

- ✓ Clocks no longer dictate your life - you merely use them as a guide, not as your master

- ✓ The earth is in more feminine balance than you previously thought. 3D is a masculine-dominated ethos whilst 4D is the feminine.

In the coming chapters we'll discover much more about how you can bring these aspects into the creation of your new lifestyle. But right now let's briefly look at how our thoughts could possibly be hindering our transition to our new world.

A Simple Lesson In 4D

I just typed $D using the upper case of my keyboard rather than 4D using the lower.

I whole-heartedly believe that my life does not contain mistakes – it contains lessons. I just have to be alert and open to the understanding of my actions followed by a moment or two to quietly ask myself what it is that I'm being told.

I take this 'accidental' typo as the universe telling me that

- I have control over my actions,
- I wasn't thinking about what I was doing,
- The $ sign indicates a metaphor about 4D not being about chasing dollars and that…
- I should not be angry toward myself or the computer for this mistake

Let's analyze this moment. On the surface it does appear to be an insignificant human action, yet it also gives us a glimpse into some of the differences between 3D and 4D.

I Have Control Over My Actions

In a 3D world, the one that we have known all our lives, we do things as a *reaction* to expectations. That is, we should do this, we're expected to be there for that, we can't be late for this, finish things on time, I must perform to expectations, don't push me and please, hurry up. We're always doing things for other people in the means and time frame that we think they expect us to have them done in. 3D is frequently all about *them*!

4D is about *me!* I have listened to both my inner soul and what my body tells me. I observed the pain and hatred and monotony associated with the third dimension and quite simply, I didn't like what I saw.

Now my inner soul and my outer body are answerable to no one but me. I make the rules about how I live and view the world. That's not being arrogant – that is simply me enjoying being me.

As a result I enjoy the most peaceful and calm journey – just as you will be able to.

I Wasn't Thinking About What I Was Doing

In my 3D world my head was always filled with thoughts, fears, apprehensions, guilt. Irrespective of what I was physically doing, my mind was frequently elsewhere planning what to cook for dinner, how to juggle three appointments at much the same time, what to give as a birthday present, how I can work a bit harder to finish this job ahead of time? I wasn't concentrating on what I was doing. I was on a treadmill, living a life dictated by the needs and expectations of others – and by the demands of a clock.

4D gives me calmness and serenity. I have time to ponder and seek understanding. I run my external human life by my inner soul rhythm and pace. My head is no longer filled with demands, concerns, expectations and time constraints. I know exactly what I am doing because I only do the things that bring me pleasure and are in accordance with my harmonious thoughts. I know that everything is happening and being revealed to me according to the universal plan for these things. There is no need for me to do several things at once. Everything will complete in its own good time. Some will observe this as selfish or arrogant, but I see that as their limited 3D viewpoint and not relevant to the truth as I live it.

4D Is Not About Chasing Dollars

In a 3D world there exists a seemingly never-ending chase for material wealth. Rarely does any one reach a happy "that's enough" moment. Rather it's all about earning, gathering, investing and then hoarding for that unexpected rainy day disaster. And does that rainy day arrive? It sure does – and more than once, because that is exactly the scenario the 3D mind has programmed and sent out into the universe. I'll work hard, be thrifty, sacrifice my happy times, be always financially diligent for I know as sure as rainbows have pots of gold at the end of them, I'll need it to get me out of a financial disaster sometime in the future. You put out that you're planning a disaster and what does the universe give you – your disaster request. It sounds to me like a guaranteed way to ensure a lifetime of missed opportunities for enjoyment.

In 4D you'll live a more natural lifestyle, taking only from nature that which you can use or enjoy that day. There's no hoarding for the future, no seeking to be richer than your neighbor, no focus on excessive money or ownership. We take nothing material with us beyond the grave, so anything that we wear, or eat or sit upon or live in or travel by is only borrowed for the time that we're here on the earth-plane. Money is simply a man-made means of transacting the sharing of goods and services. It will no longer be the dominating, all-pervading threat (or lack thereof) as it is in the 3D world. Some additional money is always useful, but it will no longer be our priority for we know that we can also use bartering, exchanging or giving things we make and grow in exchange for food, clothing etc. We will also recycle household items and clothing so that our needs are less.

Transferring Blame

I am human and therefore I continue to learn. Consequently I should not be angry toward either myself or the computer for this mistake. In my 4D world I do not intentionally transpose my ego or anger on to any other person or thing. Old habits and thought processes take a lot of effort to overcome, and after a lifetime of living these habits, I suspect I'll still continue to react to some of them – but they will become fewer. I am now alert to when and how they sneak into my life so I can quickly weed them out of my thinking, adjust the situation to a more spiritual one and learn from the experience. Each seed of ego that I catch and remove is a potentially large weed that doesn't get to grow in my 4D world.

In my old 3D world any deficiencies in my life could be blamed on others, or the lack of time, or the color of the shirt I was wearing that day. It didn't matter what I blamed – it was simply transference of my responsibility to someone or something else. I was not willing to admit that I wasn't internally happy nor was I at peace with others. If my ego couldn't make something perfect, then I'd transfer the blame. I was not taking responsibility for my own actions.

My thinking had to change!

♥ *My Action Plan*

- ❏ I can now see that it is my 3D attitude that has brought me to my current uncomfortable position

- ❏ Happiness is there waiting for my change of attitude

- ❏ I embrace the possibilities of 4D living to change my world for the better

CHAPTER THREE

I AM – LIVING A JOYOUS EARTH DAY

"The most important thing is to enjoy your life – to be happy – it's all that matters."

- Audrey Hepburn
Actress, Humanitarian 1929-1993

I've always related more strongly to a truth when I know that the writer has lived or observed the experience first-hand. I understand that if I try to emulate it, that it will not be exactly the same experience for me. As there are many variables from that original experience I know that as I read the words, particular aspects will resonate with me more strongly than others. Instinctively I know that these are the truths that I have been seeking.

Let's now look at a typical day in my life and see if there are nuggets of spiritual guidance that might also relate to your exploration. In the following chapters we'll enlarge on some of these aspects and look at wider philosophies of life.

Each morning I wake up to a joyous new day filled with potential for sharing love and happiness with everyone and everything in the entire universe. I re-affirm my gratitude and my new affirmations.

As the day progresses I continue my thoughts and expressions of gratitude. I proffer love to all. I enjoy the bounty of the earth that has been attracted to me for my enjoyment. I unconditionally share my love with both the humans and the wildlife who live within my circle and who I encounter throughout the day.

In bed at night I give thanks for my peaceful and abundant day. I reconfirm my love for all things and all souls. And in those last minutes before sleep, I confirm my "I AM" creed.

As a result I am calm, relaxed and totally as one with the universe. Therefore I sleep deeply, soundly and often with extraordinarily vivid astral traveling during my dream state.

But before we go further, a word or two about my belief in who I am.

The Hebrew Bible in Exodus 3:10 tells us that Moses, when faced with the burning bush, asks God for identification, a name. The word *Ehyeh* was used, and scholars tend to agree that the word can be translated as *I AM*. In the King James Bible it can also be translated to *I AM That I AM*.

God (or Source, as I prefer to use) is therefore the Creator, the energy, the epicenter of the entire universe, above and beyond everything.

This energy is captured in atoms and molecules. And when they cluster together we have definable shapes known as human beings, animals, rocks, clouds, tractors, fish, or whatever else is familiar to us. These clusters are not solid - there is space between each of the atoms. Our eyes see them as solid, but in reality we are all just vibrating masses of Source material.

I am therefore one of these – internally I'm an eternal soul of light, but externally I'm an energy bundle of Source material vibrating at such levels so that you and everyone else can see me as Peter, the 'solid' human being.

Therefore I know that I am physically made up of God material, the atoms of Source. I have been born from Source and in due course I will disintegrate back to the individual atoms of Source.

At all times I am connected directly to God/Source. This means that as God/Source is perfect in every way, then so am I. Always.

Hence my creed for living is *"I AM That I AM"*

- *I AM* (as an identity for myself)
- *That I AM* (that I am indeed part of God with all the same perfection).

"I AM, I AM" works just as brilliantly.

This is the single most important belief in my life – and if you get nothing else out of this book, remember these few words, and action them on a frequent daily basis. They will sustain you through any adversity, bring abundant joy, provide you with confidence and courage, and bring you the calmness and serenity that walking with the greatest ally in the universe could possibly do.

This is not new philosophy - it has been known for a very long time...

> *"All things are one"*
>
> \- Heraclitus
> Greek Philosopher 540-480BC

If this sounds fanciful to your skeptical scientific mind then I urge you to inquire into Quantum Physics where such philosophy has been scientifically proven.

You might also like to discover how all living things and all things that have lived are connected through the molecule of DNA. I recommend the BBC television and DVD series *Wonders Of Life* presented by Professor Brian Cox. In this 5 episode series he presents DNA as a chemical process that is the consequence of the laws of physics. Episode 3 *Endless Forms Most Beautiful* is the most concise and visually beautiful explanation of our universal interconnectedness that I have yet seen anywhere.

This New Age thinking that we are exploring is therefore no longer banished to the outer reaches of believability – it's an integral truth through which we can see that we are all connected to everything, everywhere and always. What a wonderful revelation for us to begin seeing a new world of peace, of sharing and co-operation.

By embracing this core belief that we are perfect – and perfectly intertwined – it becomes far easier to begin to open our thoughts to all the other possibilities available to us.

My Day Begins With …

"Good morning beautiful world. I greet you with gratitude and joy - and I send peace, love, harmony and blessings to everyone and everything throughout the universe".

Simply by awakening, I am in gratitude. I have been granted another beautiful earth day to enjoy and that in itself, is abundance fully deserving of gratitude.

I follow that with my mantra:

"I AM That I AM. I am born from Source. I live as Source. I am eternally Source. I am connected to every molecule of the universe and to every soul. I am love."

As I luxuriate in the twilight period between sleep and full consciousness, and still with my eyes closed, I begin by sending love, peace and harmony to the world, to every soul, atom and molecule in the universe. It is my way of reminding myself that I am as free of ego and its dominating effect as I can be at that time.

I then repeat my creation list - for the people, physical objects, satisfactions, money, etc that I desire to attract to me. I recite them with as much *feeling* as I can muster, and I picture them in my mind as having already been manifest into my life. I live my day from the perspective that I am already blessed with their arrival.

This is followed by a variety of gratitude moments based on whatever comes in to my head – the weather, my home, my friends and the possibilities that the new day offers.

I thank my guides, angels, healers and all others in all dimensions for being with me and for their love and guidance (this book being an example of that guidance).

With a final moment of reflection where I literally feel surrounded by both the warmth and the white light of love, I open my eyes and begin my peaceful and magnificent New Earth day. With an additional tingle of excitement I anticipate the interesting new people I'll meet, appreciate whatever the weather is going to be that day knowing that I'm part of the natural cycle of nature, and give out my love to everyone, everywhere.

It's another great earth day and I'm part of it. How fantastic is that!

The Law Of Attraction

Over the last century or more, the term 'law of attraction' has become universally accepted for describing how, through applied energy, like can attract like. What you think is what is reflected back to you. That is, negative thoughts reflect back negative qualities in your life. Conversely, what you imagine in the way of material abundance can become material reality.

Abundance/Creation List

To focus your desire for change you need to make a list of what it is you desire to attract in to your new life. Whatever you can conceive as being of importance you can add to the list. This can range from physical objects to money, a new lover to a new job, living in another location to vacation travels, from improved health to time for meditation. There are no limits. This is *you* asking for precisely what it is that is going to make *your* new life totally wonderful. There's no need to specify how it will come to you as that is the role of the universe, but you do need to be precise – in color, size, location, price range, etc.

You need to visualize it, verbalize it and believe that it is already in your life. Make it so real that you can imagine holding it, feeling it, seeing it and using it.

By making a list and then adapting and updating it from time to time, you have focused your attention on your deepest and most cherished desires that only you know about. By writing them down you can speak them out loud to yourself, or say them silently as a bond between you and the universe. You can put them in your pocket to read several times throughout the day, put them next to your computer or wherever you'll see them on a frequent basis. Your belief in seeing and feeling your individual desires as already being in your life will work miracles for you.

Your Vision Board

From personal experience I suggest that your specific abundance list can be greatly enhanced with a Vision Board.

This is simply a bulletin board with a comprehensive collection of what you are seeking in life put together in visual form where you can see it, enjoy it, reflect upon it, reinforce your desire for it and with gratitude, *feel* that it is already in your life. The things that we desire are already in existence and all we have to do is attract them to us.

I suggest that this display should not be less than a meter/yard square, as over time you will want to add photos, newspaper and magazine clippings, quotes and inspirational items. These could include a photo of your dream home, your bucket list of travel destinations, a photo of the person(s) you send healing to, that new household item you desire, the type of person you'd like to marry, the theatre show you would like tickets for, a person who inspires you to be a more loving person, a charity you would like to volunteer for, the celebration you would like for that special event coming up in your life, etc. The list is endless, but when you look at it above your desk or on your kitchen wall or where you will see it when you first wake up, it should be a nutshell view of your future - a future that will make *you* happy when all of these things are created in to your life.

As you remove an item from the board because it is now a reality be grateful for its arrival and replace it with another happiness desire. In this way you are always focused on creation. You know that you can - and will - create it in to your life - and you can already see and feel the happiness that will continue to flow to you because of your connection to everything through love.

Always reinforce your desire with *feelings* as if you are already enjoying the benefits of it being in your life. It's my belief that it's the *feeling* aspect of manifestation that really ups the vibration levels of desire and that puts out even stronger positive vibrations to the universe.

Visualize it. Feel it. Believe it. Enjoy it!

It's also my belief that because I have placed my order at the universal restaurant I therefore know that in due course, when the kitchen has finished the preparations, then my order will be fulfilled. The order remains in the kitchen until cooked and then as expected, it is served to me as wonderfully and joyously as the menu description said it would be, course by course and exactly at the right time. Unlike most real world restaurants the universal one never closes and can serve you any time of the day or night. Just be ready and grateful for when your request shows up – at whatever hour and from whatever direction!

Throughout My Day…

Throughout my day I enhance my happy and relaxed world with actions, observations, enhancements, requests and reflections.

Talking With My Guides And Healers

My life is a team effort - and always, everywhere and without exception - my unseen but all knowing support team in other dimensions, are with me. If I need guidance I simply request it. I constantly thank them for being with me. The use of a pendulum is a good method to receive answers to your yes/no questions - clockwise response for a "yes", anti-clockwise for "no".

Sometimes they give to me without my specific request. Only in the last month I was sitting in my car at traffic lights when I was rear-ended by another driver who under-estimated her stopping ability. It was a solid bump, but no damage was caused to either car. As I analyze that incident I know that it was my wonderful guides who intervened and kept my passenger, my physical car and myself safe. My passenger perhaps would not have believed in the unseen hand at work but I certainly do!

Blessing Those In The Passing Ambulance

I will not know who rides in that ambulance but it will be a person who is in need of urgent medical support. As all humans are connected to me I send my love and blessings in their time of need. It only takes a moment but it reminds me of my interconnectedness to all living beings.

Consciously Slow Down The Pace Of Living

Look back at your calendar of events for today. Can you see the speed at which you had to move in order to get them all done? Would achieving slightly less at a slower speed have helped you relax, helped you find that elusive time you were seeking for yourself? I have found that by controlling your inner speedster you will be surprised at how much happier and relaxed you become. Lessen the time you spend on your electronic tablet, cell phone, computer and/or all those social media outlets and you will also achieve a similar outcome.

Disengage With Time

Time is an artificial man-made construct devised to more efficiently organize human life - and this it does extremely well. However we must also realize that we are not slaves to its deadlines, nor should it totally control our lives – it merely gives us a framework in which to efficiently co-operate with our fellow humans.

I agree that there are time deadlines we accept or are forced upon us by external forces (such as our employer or a sporting event starting time). That our daily achievements are often measured by the amount of activities we can fit into one day (the busy housewife and mother who also works externally from the home). And that our body clock governs expected times for sleeping and being awake.

But to lead a balanced existence we need to find more 'self time', those periods each day that we set aside for our own inner quietness. To do nothing, to listen to our inner self, to play gentle music, to be as one with our surroundings – these things we owe to ourselves.

Choosing 'time out' allows us to move in to and occupy our own world of space and time, unregulated by expectations or demands from others. It's a space where we renew, replenish and repair our energies and reconnect with the infinite. It's time to embrace…

Meditation Time

Choose your own special place – within your home, within the cathedral near your city office or in a public garden, beach or forested area – but make it a place where you will not easily be interrupted.

If you choose to do it at home close down the computer, switch off the cell phone and the house phone, perhaps draw the curtains, select some gentle background music if you so desire, burn some incense, close the door to other family members – and sink into a comfortable chair and begin your contemplative time. Whatever brings enrichment for your heart, your soul or your physical body can be celebrated and whatever questions you want answered can be enquired into.

I place myself where I can have both feet firmly on the earth with my back reasonably upright, but comfortable. Each hand sits on a knee, my eyes are closed and quietness surrounds me. A pen and open notebook sit beside me ready for any revelation I need to immediately write down upon returning to earthly consciousness.

I begin by repeating my mantra:

"I AM That I AM. I am born from Source. I live as Source. I am eternally Source. I am connected to every molecule of the universe and to every soul. I am love."

And I move into a world of endless discovery. My questions can be answered, my desires are spoken of, I can see colors, I am taken to places for insight, healing and revelation. I can remain reasonably conscious of my earthly surroundings but if I am in a totally relaxed environment like my home, then I know only the visions that are presented before my third eye.

Whatever happens, I always awaken refreshed, with energy renewed, my vision widened, my thoughts cleared and my gratitude abundant for the joy and perfection of my earth life as part of a much wider universal existence.

Look upon it as your 'education' time, as a board meeting with your powerful and loving allies, as a healing time, as an insight to the endless possibilities your life offers. Whatever you receive from this peaceful time it is *your* time, where *you* are at peace and totally connected with the infinite energy stream of the universe. For ten to thirty minutes enjoy being an integral part of your eternal Source connection.

Reflection

Reflection is not the same as meditation. It's an opportunity for a moment or two to cease our constant movement and chatter to *observe* our beautiful and amazing world.

Throughout the day I reflect on its beauty, the sources of the joy that constantly fill my heart, the myriad of blessings that make my life comfortable, the wonder of life, my health, my spiritual role in bringing knowledge and love to the world, my friends, family and readers. This reflection gives me calmness and serenity, particularly as I am now more focused on the little details of life that surround me.

One of my favorite places to reflect is sitting on a park bench. When you arrive your eyes will survey the whole scene, but as you become quiet you begin to draw yourself in to the detail –

the birds hopping nearby, the spider web on the bench, the ants in a long trail near your feet, the insect on your knee.

As you go about your daily activities these moments will happen often and naturally. Smell the flower, feel the misty raindrops on your face, look at the bird singing his song to you, bless yourself for not having to live your life confined to a wheelchair, feel the clean running water from your tap, admire the stars and ponder the immensity of the constellations, hold a baby's tiny hand and imagine the possibilities offered to this new life unfolding. Such moments of reflection remind us that we are part of an intricate and immense chain of life. Send a blessing of love and gratitude before continuing on with your busy life and you will surely receive back in abundance.

For those few minutes each day we can recognize and appreciate that we are all creatures of the earth, each and every one of us perfect and inter-connected through Source.

Laughter

Have you noticed how a laugh lights up a person's eyes? How animosity is dissipated when there is laughter? How the world suddenly seems a happier place to reside in?

To me these are good reasons to laugh at the silliness of what I sometimes do; to laugh when the absurdity of the situation brings us all to a point of commonality; or laugh when the universe takes control and puts us in a situation where laughter relieves tension, changes the emotional color of the day or where there is simply pure joy happening.

Just yesterday I heard about one such moment that happened a few days before – as the coffin was being lowered into the ground a mourner 'accidentally' had his trousers fall to the ground. The gravity of the moment was lost as pure joy and laughter swept the mourners. Life was again embraced and it was laughter that gave it a kick-start.

You don't always have to look for laughter – sometimes it will find you, and in the most unexpected places. Laughter is like love – share it and feel all the better for it.

Contacting Loved Ones

Staying in contact with family and friends is best when it is seen as a two-way street. We need to offer out our desire to share with other loved ones just as much as they need to seek us out. That's the ideal, but so often we get caught up in our own activities that too much time passes before we realize that we are missing the contact.

One thing I enjoy pondering is the "whatever happened to?" thought.

Perhaps there's a name you've begun thinking about that you haven't recalled for a long while – and then "like magic" it's not very long before you hear of them, possibly meet them or in some way, have your question answered. It's the joy of creating the connection through thought and love, and then having it answered that is another positive demonstration of our interconnectedness.

Beware of the moment when the answer comes via the Death Notices in the newspaper. That's too late! If you know how to contact the person you are seeking, do it now, today. Too often I hear people say "if only I'd telephoned them a month ago when I meant to...."

Right now you have the means to share your love with them – do it! I have a life-long friend in a nursing home and I'm now enjoying the best ever conversations and reminiscences with him because I focus my diary to include regular visits to him. When you take time to care for others your life will be rich with love.

Reading Spiritually Based Books

I believe that I have lived an earthly life many times before. That I have been reincarnated as many different human beings in order to learn aspects of my quest for enlightenment. And this applies to each and every one of us.

However, we have all had our previous incarnation experiences, knowledge and memories obscured from our current earth-plane consciousness. The soul that we are, instinctively knows that it is on a learning trajectory. Therefore it is my belief that the curiosity that we have as a soul having an earthly existence is really a desire to absorb spiritual sustenance through new and enlightened experiences.

Other advanced souls, the Light Workers, have already written copious numbers of books, recorded amazing channeling talks and taught earth souls the skills to create, educate, heal and inspire. I reach out for this knowledge so that I can grow, learn and in turn, inspire others. Their words and actions are as important a sustenance for me as food is for my physical body. Each day I seek out something that interests me or will guide or alter my thoughts and actions for the betterment of all I come in to contact with.

Reading before sleep is a good time for me, as the messages stay with me throughout the night and immediately inspire me at the beginning of the new day. An afternoon break whilst enjoying a herbal tea is also good. Perhaps other times will be better for you - your journey to and from work, during vacations or whilst sitting on the beach could also be productive times for your inspirational reading.

Don't neglect this soul learning; it's really what our earth-plane journey is underpinned by. We're on the earth-plane to learn, to raise our vibrations to a higher level, to experience the wonders that surround us. The spiritual souls who write the words we need to read are advanced teachers, and their wisdom is our guiding light. If we read and learn, then it demonstrates much about ourselves – we are not drifters, content with mediocrity, but rather we are embracers of possibility, souls alive with the energies of Source. A few minutes of spiritual education every day soon compounds and will never go astray in shaping a better life for any of us.

Enjoying The Weather

Be grateful for the appropriate clothing that you can wear to enjoy it. We can't change the weather, so why complain about it? My approach is to be thankful for whatever is on offer that day, dress accordingly and simply go about my business however the weather allows that to happen. It's all just part of the fabulous life cycle that happens without any interference from man. It's natural, it would happen with or without us being present and it's quite simply the forces of the earth going about their normal business.

I find joy in the changing of the seasons - hot days, cold days, calm days, windy days, wet days; every one of these means that I get to feel different because I wear different clothing and my skin reacts accordingly. The weather offers me the opportunity to be grateful for being able to observe and experience nature in action. It is also part of me as everything in the natural world is also Source.

When you're in tune with the natural forces you do not fear them. On rainy days I often venture out of the house to undertake an errand and not get wet. In fact frequently the timing is perfect with the rain commencing again just as I walk into the house on my return. That is right up there with finding the right car space or getting the best seat in the theatre. Be in tune with Source and the world of nature, and you too can enjoy the outdoors wherever you might be.

Ignore All News Media As Much As Possible

Disassociate your self as much as possible from the 3D world of violence, argument, corruption, hate and horror as displayed in all forms of news broadcasts.

Yes, we need to have some knowledge of what is happening between the seven billion of us but we can limit that media exposure to items that might directly impact on us in some way or that can enhance our knowledge or appreciation in a positive way.

If we are to live in a 4D world of love where everyone else is part of us, we need to share that love, that humor, that respect, that humanity to make a new world order. We don't need to continually be told what others think for we are already living our own peaceful and loving journey. Nor do we need a constant barrage of reports and graphic images showing man's inhumanity to his fellow man.

It will take effort and commitment on your part - but it can be done!

You make a difference by undertaking action – that is, by switching off to the 3D world and its media trappings. Begin instead, to look inwardly to love and all its dimensions and begin to feel the difference in your life.

Ignore Advertising As Much As Possible

Even if it feels like there is no escape from these do your best to ignore their messages. Every day you will be bombarded with advertising. Even though you will see these you do not have to act on them.

We must remember that advertising is aimed at persuading the recipient to change their behavior toward the product or service being promoted. So they send out temptations to make the recipient believe that they must own or use that product immediately or else feel socially, morally or ethically out of step with the communal majority. It's saying that just because it is made then you must come and buy it. It's 'new', 'improved', 'bigger' – therefore help both yourself and the economy by purchasing. (And incidentally, though unsaid, you'll also be helping their profitable bottom line!)

As emerging 4D self-sufficient souls we live in a world where we use only that which is of immediate value to us. We grow some of our foodstuffs, we recycle clothing and furniture, ignore product updates that are produced purely for the sake of getting new sales. We seek out markets where we can purchase handmade local artisan products and locally grown foodstuffs therefore producing the lowest carbon footprint we can. We purchase, trade and bargain for comforts in our life but we don't need three of this or six colors in that, the biggest yet released television screen nor thirty plus pairs of shoes. All things within moderation is our New Age motto - and with the least harm to the earth and the most support for the people who helped make it or grow it.

Let us *desire* whatever we like – but *need* nothing other than the basic staples of food and shelter!

Once we feel as one with Source, and therefore with the fragility of the earth and its limited resources, we have a comfort zone of sufficiency that allows us to ignore the pressures of all the advertising, selecting only those items we feel comfortable with acquiring.

We also realize that we don't actually own anything, we are simply custodians of whatever we use or have around us. We arrived here with nothing but our human body and we shall leave at our passing with nothing, not even that body. Any possessions that we have the use of during our lifetime remain firmly here on the earth-plane. Why then fight each other for 'ownership' of physical items, abuse the earth's resources or gather more than we can use of anything?

With 4D insight we can see the absurdity of it all – and the false promises that advertising can offer.

Listen To Music Appropriate To Your Vibrations

I enjoy listening to music at various times throughout my day, and the type of music reflects my various moods.

If I am writing and I am on a creative roll, then my music can be upbeat with an urgency and grandeur about it. Or if it's background music to quietly inspire and relax me I will choose chanting or some other New Age music collection. When I sit and reflect it may be with a single instrument such as a panpipe – or it may be in total silence.

Music connects with something deep within us, a something that could almost be part of our DNA. Irrespective of the vocal language used it's the musical beat, the vibration that connects to us.

Why is it that we can all tap our toes to a musical beat whether we are indigenous to New York or the depths of the Amazon jungle? There's been no formal training yet instinctively we respond the same way. And when we respond we all smile and laugh and without words, we express our enjoyment of the musical connection.

Aren't we simply and instinctively connecting to Source without realizing it?

I make my day a more textured one by making that musical connection. For me a day without music is like a world without birdsong – unthinkable!

And as always, I am thankful that I have the means to play the music, to have hearing to listen to it, the money to purchase it and the heart to respond to it.

End Of The Day Gratitude Prayers

I believe that the way you end your day carries through the night to be the basis of your new day. End your day in anger and you'll not only have a restless night, you will awaken to it and it will continue to grow as the new day unfolds.

Alternatively you can take those last languid moments of the day to encourage rest and a sound sleep by being grateful. I've done this for many years and rarely do I have restless nights. Depending on your sleeping arrangements, you can express your gratitude vocally or silently as in a prayer.

I begin by repeating to myself my mantra;

"I AM That I AM. I am born from Source. I live as Source. I am eternally Source. I am connected to every molecule of the universe and to every soul. I am love."

This reminds me, as it has done so many times already through the day, that I am energy, I am love, and therefore I am as one with the all-powerful Creator or God if you will. I am not separate from this force – I AM that force, now and forever,

My routine before sleep includes reflective gratitude for all the wonderful things that included me that day; from eating good food to meeting the nice person on the bus, being grateful for the money that allows me to live comfortably, to the sunshine that warmed my shoulders. I thank the computer and the internet for my ability to communicate with distant friends. I'm grateful for my perfect health, my senses, my loved ones, the angels, guides and other entities that support me from various dimensions, the warmth and comfort of my bed. Whatever supported me in creating the happiness and joy over my day is thanked.

I run through my current abundance/law of attraction list going through it one final time for the day. As I silently speak my desires I reinforce their connection to me by *feeling* the joy that they are already with me, and already part of me.

Finally, through the joy in my heart, I send once more peace and love and harmony to every molecule in the universe, to every soul and to every entity.

Drowsiness comes easily and I sleep and dream peacefully. I astral travel to magnificent dimensions in full color and sound, I visit sources of knowledge and I discover answers to my questions. My sleep journeys are every bit as joyous as my earth bound days.

☐☐☐☐☐

♥ *My Action Plan*

- ☐ I live every day joyously
- ☐ I make "I AM That I AM" my central belief
- ☐ I give gratitude every morning, throughout the day and before sleep
- ☐ I acknowledge my unseen guides, healers and angels
- ☐ I create a vision board illustrating my desires
- ☐ I fill my day with laughter, meditation, spiritual reading, tranquil music and reflection time
- ☐ I isolate myself as much as possible from advertising, the news media and the demands of time-based expectations
- ☐ I give out unconditional love to all

CHAPTER FOUR

RELIGIONS AND CELEBRATIONS

"Gratitude helps you to grow and expand; gratitude brings joy and laughter into your life and into the lives of all those around you."

- Eileen Caddy
Author and Co-Founder Findhorn Foundation 1917-2006

Learning From Religions

So-called New Age philosophy has been around as long as there has been belief in a strong central force from which all our human needs can be met. It has had different expressions in different belief systems and therefore has been a disguised and fragmented guidebook for human behavior for scores of generations.

Have you noticed how much of what I'm saying is already part of many religions?

As humans we were given the keys to a better life centuries ago but for some reason those words of enlightenment and their deeper meanings are increasingly being lost or ignored by many. No longer are they seen as words to live by, but rather words to have to listen to as part of religious doctrine - and then let slip out the other ear without taking in and enacting their truth.

Today's New World, New Earth, New Age – whatever you prefer to call it, is simply the amalgam of the truth philosophies from all of these myriad of sources. We were given guidance for a joyful and peaceful life all those thousands of years ago, but then our ancestors took selective elements of these truths, embellished them with structure and ceremony and called them a religion – generally along the lines of *their* belief being the *only true* belief. Hence our religious wars, the control of populations and the disillusionment of large numbers of their followers.

The result is that large communities have been disenfranchised from the truths that would make their lives more joyful, peaceful and harmonious – hence the rise of New Age spirituality minus the religious trappings.

Let's take a very brief look at some of the truisms that already exist in religions so that we can see that whatever religion we might already follow there may be elements that can reunite us with the truths we are currently seeking.

Hinduism

Provides the belief for everything coming from the one Divine sacred source. Therefore everything and everyone is Divine and sacred. The Divine spirit permeates everything, everywhere.

> *"There is nothing noble about being superior to some other man. The true nobility is in being superior to your previous self."* - Hindu Proverb

Taoism

Lao Tzu in his text *Tao Teh Ching* also talks about heaven and humanity being as one, as is everything within the universe. There is a universal connecting force between any and every thing.

> *"Life is a series of natural and spontaneous changes. Don't resist them as that only creates sorrow. Let reality be reality. Let things flow naturally forward in whatever way they like."* - Lao Tzu

Buddhism

This is a belief in and practice of, a way of life that leads to individual wisdom, and in particular through love and compassion, to inner peace. By living peacefully, a day at a time, and rejecting physical abundance, we can become enlightened.

> *"In the end only three things matter – how much you loved, how gently you lived, and how gracefully you let go of things not meant for you."* - Buddha

Islam

Muslims, the followers of Islam, believe in an Almighty God (Allah) - *"He is God, the One and Only"* - and that angels, who have total obedience to God, are the communicators between God and the individual. Good earthly deeds will be rewarded in heaven. Personal communication with God, especially through prayer is an essential part of life as is living any action that is pleasing to Allah. The Qur'an is the literal word of God and is the defining document on how to live a merciful, compassionate and just life.

> *"If you are grateful, I shall certainly give you increase."* - Qur'an 14:7

Indigenous American Indian Beliefs

Centers on a belief that there is a connectedness with all matter: living, spiritual and physical. Includes respect for the abundance of the earth and its conservation for future generations.

"Everything on the earth has a purpose, every disease an herb to cure it, and every person a mission. This is the Indian theory of existence." - Mourning Dove (Christal Quintasket)

Religious Society Of Friends (Quakers)

Have a belief in the Inner Light, with a direct line for each individual to the Divine Creator. Also a world where all individuals are equal, a world without violence or wars and a world where there is social justice for all.

"That which makes a people blessed and happy is that they hear and obey the still small voice which says, this is the way, walk in it." - William Shewen 1631-1695

Judaism

There is a belief in one eternal God to whom you direct your prayers, who lives within you and to who you are ultimately responsible for your deeds. The Ten Commandments are the basis of God's laws.

"Seek the good in everyone, and reveal it, bring it forth."
- Rabbi Nachman of Breslov 1772-1811

Pantheism

Followers don't believe in an overall superior God, but rather that the universe exists in everything. The name is derived from the Greek words *pan* meaning all and *theos* meaning God, therefore equating to All is God. There is a strong integral connection to that spirituality which permeates the believers every action. They are as one with everything (particularly nature and the earth) and it is a personal soul connection that is paramount in their every action, thought and deed. Perhaps this is as close to New Age spirituality as any philosophical collective has yet expressed.

"The most precious things of life are near at hand, without money and without price. Each of you has the whole wealth of the universe at your very door." - John Burroughs 1837-1921

New Age Philosophy And Christianity

For Christians, there is a belief in an all-powerful external force that followers know as God. His only son Jesus Christ lived on earth as a man, and gave forth doctrine in order to assist mankind to live more spiritual lives. This knowledge has been collected, edited and published as the Bible.

To me, Bible quotes such as the following are in direct agreement with New Age thinking. Would you not agree?

"Do not conform any longer to the pattern of this world, but be transformed by the renewing of your mind" - Romans 12:2

"But the fruit of the Spirit is love, joy, peace, patience, kindness, goodness, faithfulness." - Galations 5:22

"For God did not give us a spirit of timidity, but a spirit of power, of love and of self-discipline." - 2 Timothy 1:7

"Clothe yourselves with compassion, kindness, humility, gentleness and patience." - Colossians 3:12

"Delight yourself in the Lord and he will give you the desires of your heart." - Psalms 37:4

"Do not be anxious about anything, but in everything, by prayer and petition, with thanksgiving, present your requests to God." - Philippians 4:6

"For I know the plans I have for you," declares the Lord, "plans to prosper you and not to harm you, plans to give you hope and a future." - Jeremiah 29:11

"I can do all things through him who strengthens me."

- Philippians 4:13

"All things are possible for one who believes." - Mark 9:23

"Love is patient and kind; love does not envy or boast; it is not arrogant or rude. It does not insist on it's own way; it is not irritable or resentful." - 1 Corinthians 13: 1-13

Learning From Christian Celebrations

Throughout the western world much of humanity celebrates the same things – Christmas, New Year and birthdays. Let's take a look at these three and discover how they already embody New Age philosophy. Perhaps we are already practicing that philosophy and don't know it.

Christmas

This is a time of year when the vibrations of the earth move upwards because there are huge numbers of people sharing this celebration. These greetings have sustained Christians for generations and perpetually do so. Unfortunately they are now often simply platitudes, to be rolled off the tongue with easy abandon and said simply because it's the socially acceptable good manner thing to do.

Consider greeting words and notice how they in fact resonate deeply with New Age thought…

"Happy Christmas" is a genuine transference of a wish that the recipient will be happier in their every day life during this

festive period. It's an acknowledgement that happiness is a state that is desirable for humans to be in. It's a reminder that Jesus came to humanity to show us how to live through love and to give us a life-plan to live our every moment by. Millions of humans have taken His birth as the event to celebrate our thanks. We've enshrined it as a time to live some of those life-skill commandments – especially love one another.

"Season's Greetings" is the bible story telling us about there being a season for everything under God's heaven. It's a reminder that our world of three months ago (the previous season) is not the same as it now is. Perhaps it is a greeting that is actually appropriate all year round and not simply for the Christmas/Holiday Season. It is in fact a quarterly reminder to embrace the new activities that a particular season brings - to embrace the new, embrace change, to adjust our type of clothing, wonder at the new and changing physical world around us. It's a reminder to be thankful for yet another cycle of the natural world in its constant change and to wonder at the miracles of Nature. And gratitude that we too, are part of this great cycle as we are all connected to all that exists in the universe.

"Spirit of Christmas" Some see Christmas as a place – Bethlehem, or perhaps as an abundant dinner table or maybe the presents sitting under a decorated tree. But there is also the

spirit that silently and quite palpably, moves through so much of the western world's population. I say palpably, as I notice that in the days leading up to Christmas among many people I come in to contact with that there is a conscious awareness that those days are different. Yes, there is a focus on getting ready for the feast days and the giving but there is also an open willingness to offer courtesy, a smile, a "Happy Christmas" compliment to total strangers.

This lightness of being is quite universal and widespread. People who wouldn't give me the time of day throughout the rest of the year voluntarily share a moment of contact with me, not in the hope of getting something back, but because they want to. This 'wanting to' seems spontaneous, springing from some deep river of hidden love within them. I enjoy receiving the compliment, and I most certainly give it back to the individual as well as pass it on to others. It's like a huge chain letter of love, a river with many rivulets rushing to fill every empty crevice. What joy there is on the earth whilst this spirit lives for the short December period! My question is why does it evaporate so quickly after Christmas Day? As the old saying goes, why can't we have (the Spirit) of Christmas all year round?

"Festive" We are not traveling the earth-plane to be unhappy souls. Our natural state is happiness, and happiness comes about not only from individually sourced delights but also

from times shared with others. Festive equates to celebration and this is achieved through sharing with others. This is a joy that is created by like-minded souls gathering together to jointly be grateful for the bounty and emotional riches of each of their lives – and to share those riches with others. Through food, music, laughter, spiritual practice, physical contact we bond with others. Together we celebrate and give thanks for the moment that we are all together in this one place and one time. Such celebrations may be brief in earth time, but at least for that period together our combined vibrations uplift each individual and together we send happiness and harmony out to the world – another droplet of love to add to the growing ocean of peace and love and harmony.

"Peace and Joy" Aspects of joy we've looked at, but peace is not restricted to the Christian world. Peace is something that is universally sought by individuals throughout most of the world whatever the culture. It's an instinct that is part of our DNA as well as an observable and relatable feeling. As individuals, we know that we want to be able to go about our own particular business without interference so long as we in turn, are not interfering with the life of others. When each of us can enjoy the freedom of movement and expression within our own particular patch of earth there is contentment. We can work co-operatively together to make it even better for us all. Deep inside us we understand that the Christmas period deserves respect and even for a few hours families stop

fighting, neighbors are co-operative and even if sometimes begrudgingly, they at least offer a verbal overture of good wishes to one another.

But it is the truce between warring factions that says so much to me. Throughout the many wars of yesteryear where there has been hand-to-hand or localized fighting there has often been a brief Christmas Day truce between bouts of fighting. There would be an understanding that the work of being soldiers and trying to kill the enemy could be put on hold whilst there were at least a few hours when weary soldiers could believe in peace, celebrate its possibilities and reflect upon the fact that whatever our religious or political beliefs we all seek that piece of the earth where we can live free.

New Year

"New Year" is in itself an expression of closure for the current time period, the year just ending.

It's where we reflect on the passing year and all of the good and the bad times, the successes, the bereavements, the happiness, the frustrations and the current position of our lives; we also take the stroke of midnight as the new beginning. There is a feeling of renewed optimism, we are for a moment in time connected in happiness to all those in our immediate company and we hug and kiss and wish each other good times for the coming twelve months. We make our lists of how we're going to improve our lives over the coming months. We feel as one with like-minded souls all around the world who are also about to celebrate when their clocks strike midnight.

The New Year offers the potential of beginning again, perhaps "getting it right" this time, of have 365 man-designated days to make sure we do. Isn't it just another way of saying welcome to a *New Age/New Year*?

"Prosperous New Year" wishes the recipient the potential that abundant money and other riches will be attracted to them during the following twelve months. By giving out positive statements like this, so it is subliminally an inner desire that we too, in turn, will also be blessed with similar riches. We believe that it's a win/win situation where we trust that good fortune will also rub off on us. How, when and if that happens will of course, have more to do with how we live our life rather than any off-hand platitude that this greeting seems to have now been relegated to. At least by saying it, it is a first-step to potential prosperity that we know is there for the asking.

"New Year's Resolution" is a stock-take moment; a time to look at where your life has reached, the implications of continuing in the same manner and if new plans are required, then these can be identified and changes put in to practice. The word 'resolution' also implies a mind-set that is positive in nature and clearly wants to see change take place for the

better. The power of that list of resolutions to be achieved will totally depend on the willpower and dedication of the owner. We know that without dedication to living our goals they will not be achieved and will wilt by the path through lack of continual nourishment. Your list can also be seen as a written version of your Vision Board and this therefore doubles the focus on what you desire to achieve.

Birthday

On the surface this is a reminder that there is a calendar day each year that is special to you - a day for sharing and happily celebrating with friends and family. A day that reminds us that the earth years are passing and perhaps it is time to give some reflection to what achievements are still to be enjoyed. Many people check their "bucket list" to review what can be struck off from the previous year, perhaps add some new desires and also imagine the joy still to come from the items on the list that will soon be realized.

And here is the essence of the underlying importance of birthdays – it's the anniversary of your birth into this earth-plane. There is a belief that we as souls choose before our arrival the nature of our life here – when we will be born, to what type of parents, when we will depart again. There is also the all-important life-plan – what we need to learn whilst here so that we can move our eternal soul on to higher vibration levels after death. On our birth this plan is locked in to a subconscious part of our memory so that we don't consciously remember it.

It's my belief that as we mature, glimpses of this DNA - this life plan - emerge to remind us what our true purpose of being here really is.

Our anniversary is therefore an ideal time to reflect on our life's purpose and observe how we are traveling to achieve what you *instinctively* know needs to be done or learned by you. It's this instinct that niggles at you. It's the chink that gives you a glimpse of what your true work here is about.

By middle age some people know that an office job isn't right for them and therefore have a complete sea-change to an outdoor job that satisfies something deep within them. Others divorce so that one of them can follow a dream. Another will return to studies as a mature age student. Some will move from the city to the country, some will discover healing gifts, some like myself, will want to write and share their words with other like-minded souls.

Whatever is annoying you as an unsatisfied dream is most likely what your true life's work is really all about – so don't dismiss it. Start to plan how you can make this achievable. A birthday/anniversary is the ideal day to begin progress in to your new life. In twelve months time you will be delighted to see the progress you've made in just that short period.

Even if it's not your birthday, make the decision to begin to flow with your destiny – right now, today! And mark the calendar for twelve months from today. You'll then be able to assess exactly how far you have spiritually traveled in that period – or otherwise!

♥ *My Action Plan*

- ❑ I realize that New Age/New Earth wisdom is as old as human civilization. I, too, now embrace this timeless wisdom

- ❑ I know that Source (or God or whatever I want to call it) is central to my life and happiness

- ❑ Through celebrations I can spread unconditional love, happiness and blessings. I can also reflect on and re-invigorate my earth-plane spiritual life and on my, as yet, unfulfilled ambitions

CHAPTER FIVE

RESOLVING SOME BIG QUESTIONS

"Our life is what our thoughts make it. A man will find that as he alters his thoughts toward things and other people, things and other people will alter towards him."

- James Allen
British Philosophical Writer 1864-1912

We all travel with baggage. It's all a question of how much.

If we are taking a vacation or a journey of some kind, we have as a minimum, a plan that includes:

- a destination and what we'd like to see and do there
- bookings on transport to get us there

- maps to help us find what we are looking for
- money, credit cards
- baggage for our clothing and belongings

How much we pack and what size bags we will need are answered by what expectations we have of the destination, what our physical capabilities are to carry it and what weight allowances our airline or other transport will allow.

Somewhere before the deadline for leaving home we must make decisions - often difficult ones - about what *not* to take.

It's a lot like that in our spiritual journey through life. Over years, maybe decades, we have experiences, collect physical and emotional items, refuse to spring clean our lives for fear of loss, all the while staggering ever onwards with no relief from the burdens.

Before we can move on, we need to re-assess our baggage and relieve ourselves of the burdens we carry with us. Let's see if we can't begin the process with a look at how we can change our *attitude,* for an attitudinal change will see us freeing our baggage shackles and allowing the free-flow of life to begin to carry us towards happiness and a lightness of the soul.

Honesty

A New Age soul always tries to be perfectly honest in their relationship with the world. You need to live a life where your soul is not in the slightest way out of balance with the natural forces of the earth and the spiritual, for if it is, you will concentrate on this to the detriment of more harmonious thoughts and affirmations you could be pursuing.

Did the store give you back too much change for your purchase? Did you travel free when you should have paid? Did you fail to return something a stranger dropped? Did you keep to yourself important information that could have helped someone?

If your conscience is pricked by an action that benefited you to the detriment of another soul, then you're out of balance with the harmony of the universe. In time you'll see the result of your action (or inaction) when it is reflected back to you. That's karma – the universal law where your actions, good or bad, are reflected back to you at some future time in equal or greater amount. Your actions today are creating your world of tomorrow. Good works equal good karma; bad actions or intent equals a similar negative response and this latter action will continue to keep you locked in to 3D thinking. (Remember, there's no karma in our new 4D world for we are now living in a world of unconditional love to all others).

Being honest is a way of life that you don't even have to think about – you just do it – always, automatically.

When you received the wrong change at the store did you notice that it was too much? But hey, the checkout kid didn't notice, you kept your mouth shut, you pocketed the windfall and left as quickly as possible. You rationalized that the store could afford to lose a few extra dollars and after all, they charge such high prices anyway. You go home. You might boast to others how you fooled the store. You try to sleep but you still have a few nagging thoughts about what happened and so sleep eludes you. The next morning you feel bad about what happened. What if the checkout kid had to make up the difference from his/her wages, or worse still, they got fired for an implication for stealing. You decide to return to the store when you can, and tell someone about it.

But the day goes on. You get busy, you forget about this promise to rectify things. By the next day you feel it's no longer an issue so forget about it. After all, no one knows it was you. You don't have to face up to anyone shame-faced about your stealing. Did you say, 'stealing'? No, that can't be you. What if the police were called? The result – no action towards rectifying the situation yet a nagging conscience that won't call it quits.

This whole scenario tells you a lot about who you are and where you currently stand on the New Age belief ladder.

You could have rectified the situation *immediately* it happened. That's what a 4D New Age person would do.

Notice how easily and naturally you could have handled the situation. And notice how that one action then developed in to your own Hollywood drama, which totally dominated your thoughts for hours and days afterwards.

Wouldn't you have been better off giving that headspace to more loving, desirable and spiritual thinking?

Dishonesty is like an attack on your soul – like a virus that consumes and clouds the purity of your being. Don't let it take up valuable mind space and set you back to negative thinking. Nip it in the bud the moment it tries to show up in your life.

Remaining Positive

If you're feeling tired and weary of life's seemingly endless burdens, then perhaps it is time to say enough is enough. It's time to begin to look for something better in the way of a new philosophy, to create a new action plan and begin living the life that you imagine is the right one for you.

This is a magnificent and pivotal time in your life as you have recognized that you no longer need the burden that has defeated you for so long. Nor do you need to continually fight against everything and everyone for your daily needs and that lack of tranquility and harmony that has eluded you.

That is the old you, because having reached this far into the book I trust that you are beginning to *know* that you can relate to at least some of the things that have been said, and in a positive way you are saying to yourself that I *can* do that. What have I got to lose?

It may feel like an epic struggle to turn your negativity into a happy, joyous, positive you. And yes, it will be a journey – but the good news is that you've *already begun* the journey. Just by relating to some of the things you've read so far, you have begun those first thoughts about the truths that the words contain. A little chink in your defenses is allowing the spiritual light to start shining through.

And you know what – it didn't hurt a bit. Nor did it take any effort, nor cost you money, nor rely on the goodness of others. No written contracts were required, no arguing took place and no one dictated the way you should think.

Your free will (that is, your ability to make totally unconstrained choices) is now reaching out to a new life with the offer of a new hope for happiness. The path to achieve that positive, upbeat and happy life you've been longing for is absolutely achievable through change of thought and action.

Yes, it really is as easy as this. Acknowledge love and gratitude and desire, and they will soon begin replacing the coldness of pessimism, negativity and lack of material abundance that has previously been the norm.

And as renewed happiness and joy come into your life so they become the normal, the natural, the life force that fills your every moment.

As we've seen already, being happy is in fact our natural state. Reach out for it and let it fill you.

Keeping Your Mouth Shut

Recognize that there is a need to practice keeping your mouth shut.

Anger, deceit, dishonesty and hate are words that are contrary to love. We are now about sharing love and harmony and peace and gratitude (I can't repeat these words too often) - and in our daily life we use words, sentences, books and conversations to enhance all aspects of love. If a word doesn't underscore love then think twice before using it. Chances are that it will contain an element of hurt for another, support for your own ego-driven ideas, imply a deceitful attitude, disapproval of another person's life path, or similar. None of this is helpful.

How often have we been in receipt of a piece of information – a secret told in confidence, an illicit observation of someone's behavior, a piece of idle gossip gratuitously given to us - that we just can't wait to tell someone else about. It's like a runaway train. It doesn't seem to matter that the end result could be a train-wreck and totally devastate the recipient - we just have to let it out of *our* system by sharing it thus making our own ego happy.

So don't do it! Think before you speak and then only use words of love and compassion. What did your mother tell you: "If you can't say anything nice about someone, then don't say anything at all."

Isn't it interesting that so many of these platitudes exist throughout the western world - and we know them quite well - yet we don't regularly use them as a creed to live by? It's time to change that.

Love Another As You Would Be Loved

You simply don't know the details of someone else's life so don't assume anything. If you do, there's a good chance you'll be wrong and you'll regret it.

Our role is to love unconditionally – that is, without judgment, malice or rules.

The whole seven billion of us are on a journey called life. Being human (and a realist), we are unlikely to get along with every one we meet, but that shouldn't stop us making it as easy and peaceful as possible for each of us to attend to our own personal needs without harming others.

We are all on *individual* journeys where we seek safe, joyful and loving pathways. We arrive on earth alone and helpless and in every instance we depart alone. What happens in between is what matters. It's a long individual journey and all of us need support, inspiration, courage and love to keep loneliness and unhappiness at bay. And love is the greatest of these.

By giving love we are not impeding the progress of another soul, rather we are offering comfort, support and affinity. This allows us to continue unencumbered on our own path. If we receive love in return (as we will if we give it first), we are doubly blessed. The free-flow of love is the life-stream we all need to be part of. Without it, we are burdened with a life journey of hardship, fear, uncertainty and doubt.

Therefore give love to your universal family of brothers and sisters just as you would like to receive it yourself. To many religious believers it's been a doctrine to live by for thousands of years. Today it is more relevant than ever.

Why Is A Particular Someone In My Life

This of course, can refer to someone you are very happy to share your journey with just as much as someone who is providing a negative impact on your life.

Whichever it is, it's important to remember that you have attracted that person through your thoughts and actions. You've not necessarily focused those thoughts on to a particular human form, but in some way you've repeatedly expressed an emotion, an action or a thought that is compatible with the result you now have.

If it's a positive relationship then perhaps you have attracted them in order to support you through some difficult decision, an emotional crisis or simply to show you through their actions, how beautiful the world is. In time, when their attachment/contribution to your life has been completed, they will move on, leaving you with spiritual fulfillment and love that will make your continuing journey on your own that much easier. Carry with you and give grateful thanks for their teachings, their laughter, their happiness, their unconditional love to you and their sheer love for life. The lessons they teach you should help shape you for the rest of your life journey.

Alternatively negative thoughts produce a negative reaction back to you, just as easily as positive thoughts bring a positive result. If you have a negative person who seems to be standing in your way or someone influencing you in a way that you feel is wrong for you, perhaps it's time to analyze your own history and realize what thoughts have been at work.

The Negative Influence

Let us do a simple exercise that will give us a better perspective on the situation. We'll make a broad list in relation to a specific negative person and then narrow it down so that those negative thoughts and emotions will stand out more clearly.

List your emotional thoughts in to two columns – one labeled *Today* and one *Tomorrow*.

The *Today* column will list how you feel right now towards this individual whilst the *Tomorrow* column will list all the desires you imagine if that person was not part of your life.

Today	Tomorrow
Anger	Happiness
Hurt	Calmness
Antagonism	Serenity
Fear	Heart-filled joy

Envy	Receiving unconditional love
Jealousy	No fear
Hate	Feeling free
etc	etc

When you have made your list, resume reading...

As you review the list it should become abundantly clear that ***Today*** has been your set of actions and/or thoughts in the past. Any of these could have led directly to the current situation. The mirror of the universe has bounced your negative desires back to you in this human form.

Your action now is to

1) Bless this person by sending them unconditional love, and stating to the universe that you bless them but no longer have need of them negatively influencing your life, then

2) Begin putting out to the universe all of those thoughts listed in the ***Tomorrow*** column.

Right now is the moment that changes your future for the positive, so there is no time to waste. Make these positive emotional desires your mantra.

This might seem silly and perhaps even hard work at first, but the more frequently you make the positive statements the quicker they will become your way of life and the new way that you view your world and other people. It's important to focus - and frequency is an ideal way to achieve this.

Don't forget to add *loving feelings* to your desires as *feeling* enhances the vibrations and can hasten the result.

As these desires become part of you, they will over-ride the long engrained negative thoughts more quickly than you imagine. It will be like learning a new language. The more that you repeat the words the easier they become, and the more readily they will become the norm. Believe that your desires are already in your life - and very soon they will be.

Change Is Constant – Don't Fear It

News headlines engender strong elements of fear when they depict natural disasters. People then begin to live in fear that some similar natural disaster is going to affect them.

Yes, natural disasters such as earthquakes, tidal waves, hurricanes, forest fires and floods do cause great human misery but we must remind ourselves that Nature and our earth are in constant movement and therefore such disasters will inevitably happen. Our planet is alive and has natural rhythms to it. As much as we try, or want to, we can't control our natural environment. This is a fact that we need to accept.

Should we build cities on earthquake fault lines? Live crowded on low-lying beach communities? Build towns that abut forest regions?

Much of our anxiety comes from the fact that we know we could lose everything we deem precious to nature's fury, but still we carry this false belief that such destruction could never happen to us.

Nature is all-powerful and as humans we will always be the loser. We have ignored her natural cycles and have paid the consequences too often. Don't live in constant fear that a natural catastrophe will happen to you and therefore let that fear limit your love of life and you actively participating in its enjoyments. Accept that change is continuous and let the fear element disappear.

Fear throws us out of alignment with the universe. It limits our possibilities. It misguides our thinking. It produces negative energy that reflects back on us as more negativity.

When you're living in a world of love there is calmness and clarity, harmony and gratitude. Why would you choose fear?

Our Place In The Universe

Much of what you enjoy, strive for, achieve or regret is based on how you view your place in the order of eternity.

Do you believe that your life here is an accidental happening? You are born, you live and you die? That's it! It is just nature reproducing itself. No all-powerful Gods, no fulfilling of pre-destined spiritual plans, no other agenda than just being in the now? Upon death you decay back to the soil?

Do you believe that you are an eternal soul having an earthly experience? That is, you've lived a life or lives before this one? At the end of each incarnation you've died, rested somewhere in the universe, been reincarnated to learn more things and now you are here before repeating the whole cycle over again?

Do you see yourself as part of a God plan, where a supreme being or force is directing and protecting you much like being a component in a giant computer game; where you become more deserving because of living a strictly adhered to moral code that has been given to humans by that force? That there will be everlasting life beyond death, and depending on how well you have performed, so your place at the eternal table will be set?

Or do you see yourself as an amalgam of all or some of these?

I do! Having been forged from that universal energy matter we call Source, I have been given gifts to use in my soul quest to rise to higher enlightenment.

Everything of the universe is part of me as I am part of it.

Internally, the real me – the soul - is eternal. It is just my physical body that is temporary and will return to a different configuration of matter once my soul pulse moves on.

I am part of an energy force that has structure and direction. I feel multi-dimensional connection to powers beyond this physical earth plane and for me that place is the star cluster Pleiades. Perhaps earth is a colony of the inhabitants of that distant place? Known since the beginning of humanity, that star-system has been worshipped, revered and spiritually connected to by indigenous peoples the world over – connections that are culturally insular without any knowledge of any other tribe or ethnic group believing the same. Why – well, that is another big question worth pursuing elsewhere beyond this book.

□□□□□

♥ *My Action Plan*
- ❏ I will clean up the amount of emotional, spiritual and physical baggage I carry in order to lighten my journey

- I will be honest, positive in attitude, loving, compassionate

- I will embrace happiness as my natural state of being

- I now understand that I have attracted people (both positive and negative) into my life by the way I think. By changing my thoughts I will begin to change my circumstances

- I welcome change as it is a natural part of all life

- I acknowledge that I am an energy force that has structure and direction

CHAPTER SIX

BE THE PERSON YOU WANT TO BE

"I, not events, have the power to make me happy or unhappy today. I can choose which it shall be. Yesterday is dead and tomorrow hasn't arrived yet. I have just one day – today - and I'm going to be happy in it."

- Groucho Marx
Actor and Comedian 1890-1977

When you sleep, is it with a clear conscience or is there anger or unfinished business within you?

You would like to make changes in your world, but you realize there are things that you need to change about yourself first?

Are you curious about finding what your real purpose in life actually is?

Then it is time to continue to get your own house in order to make way for the answers you seek.

Unfinished Business

This is like carrying an injury that will not heal. It's a pain that is always within you, every day of the year. It does not heal itself, the pain never lessens, its aggravation remains directly connected to your thoughts.

It reminds your ego that it is not in total control of you whilst this memory of an event remains unanswered. It's a burden that sits heavily on your ability to love easily and unconditionally.

It is unrequited anger – a big soul-destroying heap of misery that's getting more rancid by the day and slowly permeating and infesting all the good works you are trying to create elsewhere for your soul. It has to be dealt with – and now! Closure is required.

If this is a scenario that you can relate to then you are being limited in your journey toward love.

Several years ago in my own life I realized that I had two areas of unfinished business that I needed to resolve. Both had been sitting there for years, both just needed me to pick up the telephone and begin a dialogue with the other person. But because my ego was so strong I saw myself as the aggrieved party. Therefore I reasoned with myself, it's not up to me to capitulate. Of course, that was 3D me avoiding potential conflict whilst keeping my ego satisfied. How wrong I was.

Each aggravation was the result of a relationship breakdown.

The first was where I was seen to have been un-Christian, disloyal and morally fraudulent over an action in my life. No contact followed that event. Nearly two decades later I sent a congratulations card to this person for a special celebration. It was my own version of an olive branch. In due course a loving note arrived back thanking me for my card and the loving good wishes that I had sent. With its arrival there was an immediate thawing of the frosty image I carried within me. It was then natural to have further contact. A brief discussion of the issue ensued, followed by the restoration of civility and love that had always previously existed. He died within two years of our reconciliation.

The other was a totally unexpected telephone call from the man I introduced you to at the beginning of Chapter 1. I had not spoken to him in a decade. Upon hearing his voice I immediately felt that the period of silence had never happened. We chatted just as we had during our happiest times.

What overwhelmed me was that he'd seen an item about me on the internet and decided right there and then to pick up the telephone and see if I was still at the old number. He needed to tell me that I had been one of the most important persons in his life and that the entire last decade had been a joy because I had introduced him to spiritualism. During that decade he became a much sought after platform speaker in their churches. He was moving interstate to carry on his vital work but felt an urge to let me know of my importance to his journey before he left. For ninety minutes we talked, reminisced and shared philosophy with joyful hearts and much laughter and love.

He also died within two years of that reconciliation.

Without his picking up the telephone at that time, his desire to share his joy with me would have gone with him to the grave and I would have been the poorer not knowing that my caring had been so influential to my fellow human being. But why had I not picked up the telephone? Perhaps this was a lesson for me - and one to share with you.

With one small action and with a few words to each other, you too can instantly dissolve similar impediments to your spiritual journey. Unfinished business will mercilessly eat away at you unless you do something about it. You cannot totally love all who share the world with you if you have exceptions to the rule.

Unconditional loving from Source is an all or nothing way of living!

Today, take time to begin the journey to healing by freeing yourself from the ego-driven unfinished business that weighs heavily within you and begin to let your vibration levels soar.

Perhaps the dialing of a telephone number could be all it takes.

Address Your Addictions And Phobias

What a huge impediment to higher vibrations they can be. If a fear of flying is stopping you having enjoyable vacations in distant places what an amazing happy new life you could have if that fear were removed. Not only happiness for you, but for your traveling companions too.

If you stutter there are techniques you can learn to use to be fluent at least a lot of the time, and surprisingly, if you have the need for it, public speaking will no longer hold the fear that it does today.

You may have a fear of crowds, or small spaces, or extreme money loss, possibly an addiction to alcohol, cigarettes, drugs, prescription tablets or sex. There are many forms of addiction and many that are not obvious to others because you have skills to hide them.

You know what needs to be addressed and these can all be assisted if you are willing to take the first step. See the release of these debilitating addictions as a major step towards your new purer life in Source and you will know that when love is on your side, you'll win through.

Appreciate that these can't be eradicated or modified by your every day New Age routines – they require trained professional assistance. So today make a decision that you will seek help to overcome them. And as you do overcome them let your New Age philosophies and actions add to the endorsement of the new emerging you. Share love, express gratitude, embrace the life flow and enjoy the boundless new possibilities that emerge from your law of attraction desires.

Say Goodbye To Self-Sacrifice

I briefly mentioned this at the beginning of Chapter 1, but because it is at the heart of our loving new life it needs reiterating.

Yes, I enjoyed making the life path easier for others, but there was a hollowness within me that kept asking what's in this for me? When my Light Worker encouraged me to say "No" to requests to assist others at my own expense of time and effort, at first it was a hard thing to do. "That's arrogant of me." "I'll lose my friends." "People will hate me." And similar thoughts filled my head. When hearing me say "No", people were genuinely perplexed. This was not the Peter they knew.

My friend's simple philosophy was to make yourself *"Number One"* in your life, and everything and every one will then find their place around you. This is not being selfish, it is being true to the infinite and eternal soul that you are. It is *your* journey, *your* learning experience. You are exercising your own free will in order to experience and learn. No one else can travel your chosen path. You can't substitute. You, the eternal soul, are the captain of *your* destiny and only *you* can set the course.

I repeat: now it is *your* turn to make *yourself* the centre of *your* universe – it's never too late. It is time to live as one with Source, time to see that you are connected to the entire universe and never dominated or controlled by others. As pure love, you radiate peace and serenity to all who connect with you. You follow your happiness path with gratitude. You thrill to the energy you have within you. You create abundance in your life. You don't shirk helping others but you no longer do it to the detriment of your own needs.

Self-sacrifice is now a thing of your past. It got you into your current mess and has no future in your enlightened New Age journey.

Stop Swimming Up-Stream

When every minute of every day is hard work then it's obvious that it's time for a change. It's time to 'go with the flow'.

Life is at it's best when it is smooth and effortless.

By taking the antagonism out of doing something you move in to free flow. By accepting that something is beyond your control you let the natural forces guide you. For me, airport departures mean that the processing will take time. I accept that. Therefore I don't get uptight, angry or stressed. I know that beyond the processing procedure I will be on a plane bound for enjoyable times with distant family or enjoying that vacation I'm so keen to undertake. Long lines, security checks, forms to fill out, etc will all happen but they will not upset my internal calmness. I'm simply going with the flow without adding disruptive emotion to the events.

I used to be a control freak – not obviously, or in every matter, but I felt comfortable when I could invest energy into a situation and achieve the outcome that I desired. Yes, it was about me. And it meant that I was always meeting opposition.

When one tries to alter the behavior, outlook or actions of others you will always be met with aggression. Understandably, their free will is being attacked and they don't like that happening. Hence they retaliate. This ups the stakes in your mind and you escalate the pressure to get them to compromise to your desired viewpoint.

And so the vicious cycle continues. Eventually there is, at a minimum, festering opposition and antagonism – or at the other extreme - hate, physical violence, war.

With this scenario, no one wins – least of all you or the vibrations of the planet.

In my life there have been many group and individual 'authority figures' who for one reason or another annoyed me (that is, they weren't doing or following what I thought they should be doing). Eventually I set myself free by not fighting them any more. I allowed them to be themselves just as I am myself.

During my private moments of reflection I pictured these people and then I blessed them and thanked them for the work, often voluntary, that they did on my behalf. They chose that route in their life and now I wanted to acknowledge their work by sending my love to them. They are my brothers and sisters of the universe and as such, are as one with me. Certainly they will make decisions that perhaps I wouldn't make, but I acknowledge their efforts, dedication and skills and I continue to send them my love and gratitude.

By cutting my opposition, I have freed my life from the effort of always swimming up-stream, of always trying to prove myself as infallibly right.

Detachment (or allowing) is most liberating for it frees you from ego domination and from unnecessary consumption of your energy.

I suggest that you simply stop trying to control every one of those people you encounter in your daily life and instead send them love for being who they are. Some you will immediately bond with, others will want to control what you can do, whilst some might even frighten you.

Send love to that person or group and feel the immediate change within you. Notice how quickly love becomes a calming, peaceful and high vibration balm to your heart and mind – and how your free-flowing journey through life now continues without effort.

Love is a smile from the heart – it opens all doors.

Seek, Discover And Embrace Your Talents

What excites you? What learning comes easily to you? What action makes you feel complete? What joy do you receive back from other humans?

Answer: *Whatever it is that makes you feel good, that's your God-gift!*

We've all been given talents, expertise, learning abilities, physical attributes, friends, live in specific geographic locations or see insights that help make us a little different from our fellow human beings.

Your talents may encompass being a good mother and bringing up your child into a loving family and community. It may be intelligence that allows you to have advanced education and then to use this knowledge for the betterment of others. Your talent could be as a channel for spiritual guidance to come through you from another dimension. You may love the natural world and be passionate about preserving and caring for it. You may be a whiz with words so therefore you can write stories and articles or blogs that will entertain and inform. Whatever your specific gift(s) you have a humanitarian obligation to use them for the benefit of others and the enjoyment of your self.

To me these qualities are central to our human journey, and one of the things that make us different from animals is *recognizing* and *using* these gifts.

If you simply look at life as birth, followed by a childhood of nurturing before arrival at adulthood, then you are only looking at the readiness period.

What then makes us complete humans is our recognition of the God/Source gift and what we do with it – and this often is only recognized in later adult years.

This action sets us apart from those who choose to ignore their latent spirituality. What, how and where we exploit this gift makes us who we are during the rest of our earth life. To many it can be seen as ourselves giving back in larger measure that gift we received. It's our appreciation of acknowledging the gift that makes each of us so precious and special.

If we don't recognize our special personal and individual gift, or if we don't act on it, then we are as the animals, drifting through life just eating and sleeping and occupying a small patch of ground.

But if we embrace our gifts then we connect to a higher form of energy source and grow the gifts. The singer brings pleasure to his/her audience, the scientist explores and brings forth knowledge, the nurse brings healing and comfort, a mother raises her children, a man works a complicated machine, a poet writes words, a storyteller makes films, the bus driver delivers safety, the philosopher dreams, the athlete runs.

Whatever your gift is, recognize it, focus on it – and embrace it. Not only will you be living your God's dream but also humanity will be the better for your energies.

Remember the years are passing. If you have not found your real work as yet, keep looking and ask others about what they observe in you that could be your special gift. You *do* have a special gift and now is the time to bring that deep satisfying pleasure in to your life.

The answer is waiting *within* you.

Make Your World A Fairer And Spiritual One

If this is the feeling deep within you, then that is a calling – and you must include such action in your particular spiritual creed.

Some of us feel that sending love out to the world from our own loving lifestyle is where we fit in to the great scheme. Others burn with the desire to right wrongs, be politically active and bring other like-minded people onto the path they are pursuing. Without the activist's dissenting voice and spiritually based alternatives, those who are in abusive power will continue to abuse and live in ego-driven, materially-based control.

To the activists of this world who are seeking to return fairness, peace, love, wisdom and common sense, I say "Thank you" for following that inner call, that inner passion. Yours is a noble cause. Don't ever lose the spiritual foundations of why you undertake your actions. Add constant unconditional love, especially in the face of direct opposition, and you will succeed. The earth needs you and your numbers are increasing daily. There is a wave of such change that is ever growing and will soon turn into a tide. In the not too distant future the earth will become a much more equal, peaceful, sustainable, spiritual and harmonious place because of your efforts.

But always remember it will be love that will make the difference – not anger, violence or righteous indignation!

Understand Anger

Anger is not about the other person, it's about us, and our reaction to the external situation. We need to look inside ourselves and understand what it is that is out of alignment.

Do we always need to be right or believe that ours is the one and only truth?

Do we feel inconvenienced by a request from another person?

Are we upset because other people will not do what we expect of them?

Do we feel emotionally or morally degraded because of their action or request?

Do we let political or religious powers rule our lives?

These are typical of the questions we should ask ourselves when we are quick to anger, or defending ourselves and our lifestyle, culture, religion or sexuality. By letting anger rule us we are simply continuing the established cycle of hate, intolerance, impatience and emotional insecurity.

It is time to step out of that cycle and take a whole new approach to life. Begin to put anger outside of and beyond your daily life.

By sending love to everyone (and that especially includes people who you currently identify as meddling, evil, hostile, misinformed) you are isolating yourself away from that vicious cycle. You now live in a world of our own choosing - of calmness, gratitude, joy and peace.

Make that choice right now and begin your new path.

Don't ignore *unconditional* love – it's the key to the new reality you've been searching for!

□□□□□

♥ *My Action Plan*
- ❑ I begin taking action on the 'unfinished business' aspects of my life

- ❑ I begin taking action to cure my addictions and phobias
- ❑ I have already begun to say goodbye to self-sacrifice
- ❑ I am enjoying 'going with the flow' rather than swimming against the current
- ❑ I seek, discover and then embrace my unique Source/God-given talent
- ❑ I actively work towards a fairer and more spiritual world
- ❑ I actively undertake to eliminate all anger from my life

CHAPTER SEVEN

CREATING MATERIAL ABUNDANCE

"We lift ourselves by our thought. We climb upon our vision of ourselves. If you want to enlarge your life, you must first enlarge your thought of it and of yourself. Hold the ideal of yourself as you long to be, always, everywhere."

- Orison Swett Marden
American Inspirational Writer 1850-1924

In this chapter let's look at the law of attraction in more detail.

Thought Creates And Attracts Abundance

Thought is vital to us if we are to change our life for the better. Firstly, we need to know what it is that we desire, and secondly, we can then use those visionary thoughts to create and initiate an action plan.

We create the desire, put it in to words, and then through action, belief and energy the abundance flows.

There is interdependent energy and action at work here. The bonus is that the more action that is created, the greater the free flow will be - with the end result being even more abundant, happy and creative than first imagined.

In reading this book you will get a lot of ideas. You'll choose the ones that resonate best with you. These in turn, present you with new thoughts. But there is little use in just having thoughts if you don't act upon them.

Begin by putting the law of attraction into effect by:

- Clearly focusing on your desires, knowing that unconditional love is your action plan

- Filling every waking minute with action thoughts, desires and mind pictures, all the while generating love and gratitude

- Believing that these desires are *already manifest* in your life, and living from that perspective

- Picturing yourself living every aspect of the life you are creating.

Remember the vision board we spoke of earlier? If you haven't made yours yet, begin it now, for your new life *is* waiting for you!

But it takes *action* and *consistent positive thinking* to bring these desires into fruition, not just acquired knowledge.

As we learned earlier - don't only be a collector of knowledge, be a practitioner of *action*!

Money

Be conscious of the fact that

a) Huge volumes of money exist in our world and it is there for you to attract should you so desire

b) Money is simply a medium of exchange for goods and services (it's just a piece of printed paper or a bit of alloy that has no value other than what we mutually want to give it)

c) No matter the amount of money you possess when you die not a cent, euro or peso will accompany you on your soul journey, and

d) You need to identify how much is 'enough'?

I have a friend now in his seventh decade who rarely in his life has more money than will pay his next rent bill and put food on his table, yet he lives an amazing life. He travels frequently, attends concerts through the generosity of friends, spare tickets and opportunities for free tickets, enjoys guaranteed government living assistance, shares his gifts of massage and counseling with all around him and in all ways embraces life's possibilities to the maximum. He has such a strong belief in the universe providing for him that indeed it does.

He always – yes, always – lands on his feet when something goes amiss. His is a life that is lived almost without money. He would be the first to embrace a financial windfall, but it would simply be a means to enjoying today even more than he normally would. He is the finest example of living every day to its maximum that I know.

Then there is the fearful – a person who simply can't recognize when enough is enough. They have a fear of destitution in their old age and in their view the only way to avoid that becoming a reality is to have so much money that they can buy themselves anything they need - security, comfort and medical care. They are reluctant to spend money which could bring them joy and happiness today. Their scrooge mentality is a barrier to their joy. Will they ever discover the unconditional enjoyment that their money could bring? I doubt it, as fear attracts fear. Just as focusing on potential poor health does nothing towards attracting positive health, so hoarding money rather than spending it on creating and living a joyful life can potentially lead to social isolation and lack of friends.

Money should circulate. Keeping it tucked away is like keeping compost without putting it to work in the garden. It will eventually become unbearably smelly and do no one any good. Invest your money into helping others or whatever brings you joy and happiness today. The more you focus on the good that money does, the more it will be attracted to you. Circulate it (without being too frivolous) and not only will you live abundant joy but don't be surprised to see your monetary wealth continue to increase. As to whether money will buy you freedom and happiness, that will depend on your thoughts and desires and how you share it around.

Say 'Yes' To Maintain The Flow Of Abundance

You've asked the universe for certain physical objects or people to show up in your life. You firmly believe that your request will shortly be delivered exactly as you requested. All you know is that it *will* appear and be brought to you. In the meantime you continue on with life.

What you don't know is how, when and with whom it will arrive. But based on my experience, you should be prepared for it/them to arrive in your life in a way that you can't imagine. And for this to happen, sometimes you have to do your part by leaving your comfort zone at home and begin mingling with the world so that through your actions you can be in the right position to coincide with what or whom you desire.

Therefore

a) Say "Yes" to invitations, and

b) Describe your desires to as many people as possible.

It's extraordinary how often the answer to your request is within the means of someone you already associate with.

For the universe to connect you to your desires you should be willing to meet it halfway, and that means that sometimes you need to be drawn to the point of where that object or person is going to be. If you say "No" to invitations you may miss seeing your desire fulfilled.

Always expect the unexpected, for the answer may be disguised and come to you from out of left field. Should you receive an invitation to go somewhere, or do something unusual, take a chance and accept it, for it is likely that the universe is getting you out of your comfort zone in readiness for a wonderful new experience.

"Their uncle knows so-and-so". "I was just reading about that yesterday". "I'd like you to meet my friend so-and-so". A garage sale offers the very item you desire at a bargain price.

A delayed flight gets you talking to a stranger who knows the answer you seek. The radio plays an appropriate piece of music suitable for your home movie soundtrack. You pass a 'For Sale' sign and you realize it's the new home you've long desired.

The answers are all waiting for you to show up.

So speak your desire to yourself as well as to others, look for positive indicators and be alert for the result you desire. The law of attraction is that easy – and it doesn't cost a cent!

Before the internet I spent some fifteen years searching the record shops of the world in vain looking for a particular piece of out-of-release music I'd heard on the radio. I believed that I would eventually find it, but where? After those long unsuccessful years a close friend was selling the contents of his home and invited a mutual friend (who knew of my desire) to see if there was anything he might like to have. Among the records there was the music I sought.

But I had missed all the clues for those fifteen years. The music was recorded in France – and he was a total Francophile. He had a scholarly knowledge of classical music, a huge collection of recorded music – and yet I'd failed to mention my quest to him. All I had to have done anytime over those fifteen years was to articulate my desire – and instantly it would have been mine.

Yes, sometimes the solution is right under our nose and we can't see it. Never make any presumption about whether someone can help you or not, as you can almost guarantee that the law of attraction says it will be the least likely person or place that you can imagine who will answer your request.

And sometimes *you* are the one with the answers for someone else. A friend of more than twenty-five years has occasionally talked about a person he knew many years ago. But this time he mentioned a surname. Immediately I was able to say I know of that person. Thirty years had passed since their last meeting but now I was able to provide contact details as well as both recent and old photos – all because of one extra word being mentioned, his surname.

So if there is an answer you are seeking, keep talking about it, perhaps enlarge it by a word or two, and you could indeed be connected to the answer by someone already known to you. I live in a city of millions, yet here is proof that connections can happen within my own group of friends. Don't be amazed, rather take it as proof of how we are all connected and that we are all one with Source. It's another example of the law of attraction in action.

Therefore give of your unconditional love, totally *believe* that your desires will be fulfilled (or better still begin living your life knowing that they have already been fulfilled), share that desire with others and then marvel at the result.

Expect nothing less than wonderful!

If In Doubt, Test Yourself

If you are like me you have recently been overwhelmed by the number of law of attraction, get rich now books that stare at you from bookstore shelves. That's not necessarily a bad thing, because I for one, like to be constantly reminded to bring my desires back in to focus. Each new book re-invigorates my enthusiasm for New Earth living and loving, and reinforces the validity of my law of attraction desire list.

When I first started to enact the law of attraction I would studiously put my desire list out to the universe multiple times a day – and then for some reason I would get diverted with another interest in life and the intensity of my desires would therefore dwindle. My desires didn't go away – they just didn't get enough focus.

Nowadays the best reminder for me is when I see another small, time-sensitive desire come in to my life. That spurs me on with a confidence that the law of attraction really does have something going for it. When you can see some evidence, you too will be a convert.

Take this recent example; on day one I set a goal before going to sleep that tomorrow $100 would come to me before I went to sleep again that following night. No conditions, no particular means, just $100 worth of value to me. By 10am the next day I had obtained three times that value. In my morning emails were details of a special vacation I'd heard whispers about and now here was the promotion. Because of the time difference I had fifteen minutes before the company on the other side of the world closed up business for the day. I telephoned, booked my journey and was told that I had a $300 loyalty credit because I had traveled with that firm previously. Would I like the credit applied to my booking? Sure would!

Such confirmations of the power of the law of attraction constantly boost my positive thinking and my use of it. My doubts get fewer and fewer the more often I see it in action. I benefit, and so will you.

Give it a try; seek something smallish and within a limited time frame – perhaps a car space at the front of a busy shop or receive a phone call from someone you've been thinking about but not heard of for a long time. Confirm it again just before going to sleep, as I believe that whilst we are asleep wondrous connections are made throughout the universe on our behalf. Go about your normal daily business but be ready for a response to your desire.

And when it arrives, perhaps in a different package from what you might have expected, don't be surprised if your response is something like "isn't that just fantastic".

Indeed, it is life-affirming knowledge to know that you are now connected to every one and every thing, and that you *can* manifest abundance and joy whenever you so desire. It's like coming home to the happiest and most contented place you can imagine.

More About Practicing Manifestations

Moving in to the 4th Dimension and beginning our new spiritual life is somewhat akin to being born again. There is much that we have to learn to replace the life-long attitudes and thought patterns that are still so evident in our behavior.

In the area of manifestation it's no longer about requesting from the head and the ego, it's about manifesting through the heart.

Manifestation is about a belief that if you can conceive it then it is already in existence within the universe and all you have to do is connect to it and attract it to you. Living your life in the 4th Dimension has already connected every molecule of you to every other molecule that exists within the universe. The energy of every one of those molecules means that they can connect with one another and create energy patterns we might call form or shape. In due course they show up in our life, perhaps in the shape of a house, or money, or furniture. It's simply quantum physics in action.

You *can* manifest, wherever and whoever you are. There are no special powers needed, no higher education required – just desire, energy, belief and an unconditional loving heart.

Let's take a look at another affirmation: *"Within 48 hours I will materialize a blue flower in to my life."*

Blue flowers are not so common but following your affirmation you might begin to look into gardens expecting to see a living blue flower. But don't be surprised if it appears as a painted flower in a window display, or a television documentary about the peony flower of China or in a ladies broach you spied in the thrift store.

This example tells us that we can indeed connect to the universe and materialize something that is outside our normal daily experience and normal expectations. We requested an observation and it was granted. A simple example like this one is an excellent learning and confidence boosting exercise that we can repeat multiple times a day over multiple numbers of days.

But perhaps we would like something more tangible in our hand. After gaining experience like the above, we can begin to become much more precise.

My Affirmation: *"Within 48 hours I will materialize in to my hand a long stem living blue flower bud."*

This is much more specific. If you are feeling the need to push the possibilities somewhat further and give the universe a more difficult exercise then this is entirely wrong thinking. We know that anything *not harmful to another living soul* can be manifest, whether that is an item small or large, in your hand or somewhere else. There is no scale of difficulty for the universe, so don't fall in to the trap of trying to challenge the law of manifestation by pushing it until it might fail. That, my friend, is a giant step backwards into 3D thinking. Can you hear yourself adding "well, I didn't get what I asked for so it must have been too big a request. I knew it sounded too good to be true. Sure, I can manifest the little stuff like a parking space, but when it comes to the really important stuff like the million dollars I asked for – nothing!"

Can you hear the anger, disbelief and self-centered ego in those words? It's a 3D way of thinking and it's not coming from a loving heart. Your earnest efforts towards total belief in being able to manifest have again been scuttled by the ego that refuses to be beaten. Don't let it!

Quite simply, we don't *need* anything and that's what our ego-driven 3D thinking can't understand. It's our *desires* that we want to manifest and that is 4D. *Need* does not equate to *desire*.

So now let's add some more 4D thinking to our example...

My Affirmation: *"I am peace and love and harmony and as one with all the universe. When I visit my friend in hospital in 48 hours time I will be carrying a bunch of blue flowers, the color symbol that will mean so much to her at this time in her recovery."*

Notice how we have been specific with time, but we have transferred the manifest from wanting it for ourselves to that of another soul who would appreciate the gift perhaps more than we would. In this case we are the instigator and then the intermediary bearer of the gift, a link in the chain of getting such a personal gift to our friend. Not only are we giving the gift of love through manifestation, we have been very specific in color, size and the fact that we *will* be carrying them. In our thoughts and heart we already have them - it's just that we don't know right at this moment how or where they will come into our life – but we *know* they will. Through the flowers we are also giving love and healing and optimism for a speedy recovery. We're thinking of others and sharing our friendship with them.

In this example, we can expect to 'discover' our flowers within the required 48-hour time span and we will have them in hand to personally deliver to our friend exactly as we desired.

You *Are* A Creator

You can use words like manifest, attract, affirm, bring to, invite, desire – but the word I use is *create*. That's a reflection on the way I look at my world and what works best for me.

Don't abandon those other words as your expression of bringing a better world into existence for you and your loved ones. If you are getting good results and your life comforts are improving then you may be happy to remain with one of those other popular and proven words. It's a totally personal and fluid approach.

Create can have many interpretations, from artistic flair to making a cake. For me it's a word that involves *action* on my part (that is, energy) which then connects with other energy that I'm seeking, which in turn leads to a positive result for me.

My interpretation of me being the creator is in the broadest sense of the word.

I determine to *create* aspects of my life that enhance my day but are not always material. Take today for example and the variety of manifestations I created:

- I created a parking space exactly where I requested in a busy shopping area

- I walked in to my usually busy hairdresser and discovered it was empty. The staff were awaiting my arrival

- I created time in my diary to visit an elderly friend in nursing care

- I desired and received an easy free-flowing road trip to see him along what is usually a stop-start chaotic traffic environment

- I was grateful for the elements of food, electricity and an oven coming together so that I could create the evening meal

- I was grateful for the previously created income that enabled me to purchase the DVD I watched after dinner

- I created new friendships and acquaintances on the internet in areas where like-minded people shared a common interest

- I created time for myself to meditate and to spiritually connect with the universe

- I spent time creating in my mind additional desirable things that I would like to have in my life

- I created a tranquil and harmonious home atmosphere

- And before sleep I will create time to express gratitude for this glorious day and to place my desires to the universe for other things I'm interested in attracting

Creation and gratitude is therefore an entire day of living and not just asking for the big items of abundant money, a better job and happy relationships.

The Keys To A Better Life

I cannot emphasize too much that abundance and joy through creation or law of attraction is based on *knowing* that you are born of Source, you are living Source every moment of your existence and as such, you are connected to every other aspect of Source – that is, every molecule in the universe.

Source means that you are perfect energy and as such you are part of everything and everyone else. Energy attracts, and therefore as energy you want to attract more energy that has already formed into another configuration. Perhaps you want money, a new cell phone or a car. Therefore an image of that item is what you create in your mind and send out to the universe. Just like placing an order at a restaurant or an online shop.

But as a creator you can do much more that just bring physical objects to you. You can begin to live in a peaceful and harmonious world of your own where you create the ambience and smoothness by your thought. Let the storm and noise and demands of 3D life swirl around you without getting involved, or even noticing. You begin to make your own patch of harmony where you are happy to exist.

Certainly we still need to live lives that involve all our close 3D friends and family, but we can do that without becoming gripped into their 3D thinking.

When they are talking disparagingly about others, let us withdraw from the conversation and say nothing whilst we send love to that person being discussed.

Let us not get involved when they take anger out upon themselves by blaming anyone else for the woes caused by traffic, something not cooking as quickly as it should have or the wine they forgot to cool before serving.

Let us be tolerant towards the heatedness of argument that can result from religious, political and cultural discussions.

We are now living in a peaceful, calm, abundant and loving world we created for ourselves and we gain nothing by joining in the persecution of others. We therefore remain silent and send love and peace to all.

♥ *My Action Plan*

- ❏ I change my thinking in order to attract money, material abundance, happiness and joy

- ❏ I demonstrate to myself that I can use the law of attraction to work for my benefit

- ❏ I now appreciate that manifestations of all sizes will become an integral part of my every day life

- ❏ I know that I can create into existence a peaceful loving space of my own

CHAPTER EIGHT

ENCOURAGING GOOD HEALTH

"If you have zest and enthusiasm you attract zest and enthusiasm. Life does give back in kind."

- Norman Vincent Peale
Minister and Motivational Author 1898-1993

Exercise

As you begin to move in to your new spiritual life it's important to also include an action plan for your new healthy body.

Doing exercise is not all just about grunt and the muscular body benefits. It's also about nurturing oneself through a quiet undisturbed think time – "me time". When you disconnect with the demands of your lifestyle and free up your mind for an hour or so, it's surprising what answers will pop into your head in regards to questions you have been thinking about earlier in the day. I always have a notebook and pen in my gym shorts to immediately write down whatever comes to me. Normally I take about eight minutes to walk to my gym and during that time I begin to ask my silent unseen guides and helpers for answers to a particular problem. For me it's often about my writing.

I enter the gym, change into my workout gear, put my street clothes and my cell phone into the locker and begin the workout. Even though the gym might be busy I workout alone, so my thoughts are not interrupted and as I peddle on the bicycle or lift weights, inspiration is free to enter my consciousness. If anything does come I write it down. If it doesn't then I simply mind-drift and cherish the hour all to myself. By the time I get back home I invariably have a couple of small pages of notes and answers.

Undertaking some exercise most days is critical to improving your good health. Go for a long walk if the structured format of a gym is too difficult for you. Or ride your bicycle.

I'm also impressed to know that current research is indicating that all we actually need to do to get and stay fit is three thirty-second bursts of intense cardio activity, three times a week. That's a total of only four and a half minutes per week! Yes, it seems highly likely that all those seemingly endless hours of sweat and effort might not be doing the participants any more good than those few intense minutes. UK and Canadian research has a way to go to prove this, but it's an exciting possible breakthrough. It also seems that a cup of green tea immediately after such an intense workout could help continue the benefits of fat loss from the exercise.

Many gyms also offer inclusive free classes in yoga, tai chi and other meditation streams as well as the traditional strength and fitness ones.

Some gyms are also moving to being open to members 24/7. Not only does that mean you no longer have an excuse for not attending, it also means that you can choose quieter times to enhance your internal experience.

In your journey to a new and happier lifestyle, don't overlook the benefits of a healthy body. When you feel energized, the world also seems optimistic and more balanced. It's a feeling that underlines my positive outlook and gives me the solid foundation from which to springboard my day. I love having that secure feeling.

Eating Pure, Natural Foods

These are foods that have not been processed very much, if at all.

As a 4D soul I respect my human body. I chose it before I came to earth, it is my only means of existing on this planet, it envelopes me, it protects me. Therefore I have a lifelong working partnership that I need to nourish and respect.

The automated side of my body is programmed to carry on without my soul's interference. Through DNA it inherited an inbuilt instruction manual. My soul-driven input gives the body additional instructions as to what I would like it to do beyond just existing and because I see my body as my best friend, I am always alert to its needs.

Do you 'hear' your physical body telling you things? I hear from it when there is pain that needs to be corrected, when it is being force-fed too much of the wrong foods, when medicines require balancing, when I'm cold, when I'm dehydrated, when there is potential danger, when the sun is burning my skin, when my body seeks sex and so much more.

When I am in balance I am greatly rewarded with perfect health, lots of energy, restful sleep, bright eyes and surprisingly few viruses that otherwise sweep the community. Keeping that balance and high body vibration levels means eating fresh natural foods (raw whenever possible), little sugar, limited caffeine and alcohol, limited fats, some exercise to a puffing stage on a regular basis and if you are an aging adult then include some weight training – and don't forget the self-recognition factor that declares that I am Source and therefore perfect.

I begin my day with a glass of water into which I have squeezed a fresh lemon. Lemon juice within the body is alkaline therefore this assists in balancing my acid/alkaline pH levels. Various herbal teas (particularly green tea) taken throughout the day also help. In the Western world our diet tends to make our body very acidic, which is not good for our health. By encouraging a better balance towards the alkaline then our body vibration level will improve − and that means greater freedom from disease and illness.

You'll need to experiment and seek medical advice as to what the best levels are for you.

Eat Something That You Have Grown

Our DNA connects us in some way to the bounty of the earth. Putting our hands into the earth is a fulfilling and deep-rooted emotional experience. Even running your hands through the warm sands on the beach is a primeval moment.

However planting into freshly turned garden soil can be one of our most satisfying moments. Through this symbolic act it's an opportunity to give back to nature and demonstrate that we take our human obligation to always keep and maintain her beauty and bounty very seriously.

Pull a carrot from the soil, pick a strawberry, reach for an apple – and then eat it seconds from where it was grown. Can you feel it? There's a satisfaction, a taste that says real flavor and 'freshness'. It's that freshness which is actually the energy of life completing its cycle from bountiful earth to human vitality.

We city dwellers have had our senses dulled by the dissipation of that life energy, that freshness, because we eat food so many hours, days or even months after it is picked. How many of us have a desire – nay, a burning need - to have a window box of mixed herbs, a tomato plant in a pot or a tub of ripening strawberry plants? No, we have not forgotten our connection to nature.

Now, take another bite of your freshly picked vegetable or fruit, close your eyes and give whole-hearted gratitude for your re-connection to the vital energies that run throughout our magnificent Mother Earth. What a wonderful blessing we have to enjoy as we recognize that we are as one with this energy!

We live integrally with all of the natural forces of the universe and this joyous moment tells us that simply by eating and appreciating a freshly picked fruit or vegetable that we have not forgotten that we are part of the totality of everything.

Go on – have another piece! When did anything else ever taste this good or this fresh?

> *"It is health that is real wealth and not pieces of gold and silver."*
>
> Mahatma Gandhi 1869-1948

Embrace Source

As my dear late mother would often state…

> *"You are nothing without your health!"*

My health is my priority in life, for everything else is more difficult or impossible if you haven't got the solid basis of good health on which to build.

Good pure fresh-as-possible food, vitamin and mineral supplements, modern medicine, alternative medicines, healing therapies etc are all wonderful in their own way to supporting and maintaining good health - but my preference is not to need them. I want 100% perfect health – nothing less. That's my mantra.

My belief is that I am born from Source (that is, God), I am Source and that Source is perfect. Therefore being I AM, I am perfectly healthy! You begin to realize that you have been the only one who has been keeping perfect health from you.

You don't abuse Source (or your God), so why then abuse your body? Once that simple fact is established within you, then keeping your physical body healthy and happy is a snap. It will not take you long to figure out what is best for *your* body. Your weight and your faculties will be stabilized, you will rid your cupboards of junk food replacing it wherever possible with fresh, natural and unprocessed foods - and you'll never abuse your precious and fantastic body ever again.

Embrace Source - and you can say goodbye to poor health.

For me, as long as I keep my vibration levels high, then disease has no ability to enter my cells. I look at a high vibration level as a great insurance policy for a healthy life.

Therefore obtaining an optimum vibration level for my physical body is my goal. At any level above 62 megahertz I will have reached perfect health in this earthly dimension.

Research by Dr. Royal R. Rife, M.D. (1888-1971) scientifically proved that at vibrations lower than 62 Mhz various diseases can begin to flourish – flu creeps in at about 57Mhz - and when 25Mhz is reached then death can be imminent.

How will you know when you have reached these optimum vibrations? By your perfect health!

It's early days for me in this aspect of my belief system, but I assure you that my aches and pains are few, common viruses rarely disable me, my energy levels are higher than in previous years, my step has a spring in it, my sex life is that of a younger man and I have a zest for life that is leading me to undertake and enjoy those things that were once piled in the 'too hard' basket.

After a lifetime of taking my body for granted, these changes for the better are a sure sign that good health is achievable through positive thought and considerate intake of foods and other supportive products and regimes. I'm not there yet, but the early results are nothing but brilliant.

I constantly give thanks for this awareness that I am Source and that through Source I can easily embrace and enjoy all of the other aspects of life that I desire. I can also see that by lifting one's physical vibration level that disease as we know it, could begin to disappear from our planet.

Begin embracing Source today and you have everything to benefit.

Our Second Brain

Another area of health research that will prove itself in due course is the emerging knowledge that we have a second brain located in our stomach area.

Its scientific name is the Enteric Nervous System. Early research indicates that it is responsible for a great amount of our happiness because a majority of our serotonin (the 'happiness drug') is manufactured there. It is also the centre for our emotions. When you have a 'gut feeling' for something, then it is probably your second brain sending you that message. In times of fright you have a 'gut reaction'. When you are nervous there are 'butterflies in the stomach'. These are also connected to this second brain area. Some researchers even think that it may control more of our emotions, reactions and happiness factors than the brain in our head. Perhaps our New Age desires for calmness, harmony and happiness can all be centered in this area.

Yes, there is still much to learn about ourselves!

Embrace Holistic and Complementary Health Therapies

Natural medicines and body meridian alignments have been known (especially by devotees of Asian medicine), practiced and proven over scores of centuries. These 12 meridians are vital, yet invisible lifelines to all parts of the body. They carry the energy streams (called Qi which is divided into yin and yang) to keep us physically and psychologically healthy. If any of these become out of alignment inferior health along that meridian soon follows.

Today the best of these 'alternate' therapies are available in most neighborhoods. They may or may not be a replacement for modern mainstream medicine but there is little doubt that in the hands of experienced practitioners we can usually benefit from their expertise.

There is massage for muscle relaxation; yoga for spiritual connection; kinesiology to re-align our charkas; acupuncture and acupressure for pain relief; herbal mixtures, reflexology, aromatherapy, hypnotherapy, meditation, cell salts, crystal healing and many more modalities.

You may 'feel' directed (that's your body talking to you), to one or more of these practices as being able to assist you in prevention, management or cure. Choose what you instinctively feel is right for you, add your positive belief in their ability to help you and then benefit from their application.

Nothing of course, takes the place of connecting yourself to Source, living as one with Source and knowing that your body is indeed always total Source. When this is totally embraced you can expect nothing less than perfect health. Don't be a doubter who uses their free will to deflect and negate the possibilities on offer.

Begin your journey to health today by seeking your own independent medical and psychological advice and start embracing the possibilities.

Walk With Nature

Be as one with the natural world.

Walking on the bare earth where you can be surrounded by the natural physical world, its vegetation and the sky, is a privilege and brings enormous benefits to our soul. It doesn't have to be just in rural areas – suburban streets and parks can be filled with trees, grasses, lush vegetated flowering gardens, small lakes, birds, seasonal vegetation changes, breezes, insects, bushes and blue sky.

Walking connects us to the natural world. Our senses have affinity with it. Our eyes see color, our feet feel the grass beneath them, our ears hear the birdcalls, our skin the breezes that skim by and our nose smells the flower perfumes. Our heart appreciates the pace of the exercise as our physical body moves beyond sedentary. You, the soul, feel both an affinity and a lightness of spirit. There's something about all of these sensory ingredients coming together that makes for a connection, a knowing that we are as one with all of nature and that our own life is in synchronicity with the natural rhythms of Mother Earth.

It's a feeling of being 'Home', and it is a feeling that we will never tire of – for we are indeed as one with Source, with the life-stream.

As we recognize the perfection of the natural world and all its associated beauty, so we also recognize the delight of being a living part of it all. We instinctively know that we are being carried along with the Life Force. We are no longer fighting against that river as we try to force our way up-stream.

Instead we go with the flow towards a destination downstream, wherever that may be taking us. We peacefully float, swirl occasionally in the eddies, avoid the rocks and see around us the sheer majesty and beauty of a world we now have time to admire and wonder at. Every corner gives us a new vista on our way to a Nirvana we are still unable to fully imagine. This is river cruising for the soul.

Bless Your Home With Fragrance

If you already use aromatherapy in your home and workplace, then you understand the power of aromas to engage with your inner soul.

Whether these are for relaxation, pleasure, emotional relief, healing, sexual stimulation or making you feel more beautiful, they should be part of your day.

Just a week ago my gym began using a vanilla scented candle at their reception counter. It's been amazing to observe the difference this one candle is making. As they arrive the members, both male and female, are noticing the rich aroma and stopping to comment on it. It's become like a silent blessing and a very welcoming gesture from the management. This is just a small example of what one scented candle can achieve to alert the world to our spiritual needs.

Add essential oils to your home. They are not only beneficial to you they will do the same for family and for any guests who visit you. Purchase or borrow a book about aromatherapy and then with your own particular conditions in mind, consider adding appropriate oils to potpourri, your incense burner, perhaps adding a drop to your pillow or to your bath water.

Anywhere that you would like better ambiance or healing burn a scented candle. You can buy delightful flameless battery-operated ones so there is no danger of fire. As they heat they release their enhanced fragrance. I use one on my desk whenever I write.

You might like to investigate the healing properties of essential oils. From arthritis to stress, insomnia to headache there are oils that could benefit you. For example there's neroli for improving circulation, sandalwood for tension relief, ylang ylang for insomnia, patchouli for dandruff and cedarwood for acne. Many are used in combination with one another; some are directly applied to the skin, whilst others are inhaled. So do your research first, find the best combination for your particular needs and then apply them to your life.

Dismiss any derogatory comments you may receive from the non-believers in your friendship or family circle. *You* know that the oils are helping you and are an outward expression of your connection with love and perfection.

After a period of use there will be some people who will notice the positive changes in your demeanor. They see a happier, more relaxed you and they also smell the aromas in your home or office. They will begin to ask you questions, for they appreciate that something is making a marked difference to your enjoyment of life.

Silently recognize that they have been sent to you for you to teach them, to introduce them to the values and philosophies in this New Age, New Earth lifestyle. In your own way you are a Light Worker, and here is your opportunity to help bring another soul to inner peace. Embrace the opportunity, share your new knowledge and fulfill your destiny as a teacher and as an example to others.

Use Eco-Friendly Products

Are the cleaning products – the washing-up liquids, the floor cleaners, the dishwasher powder, etc - you currently use, toxic chemically based? If so, then as you use them and dispose of them, they are finding their way into the ecological systems of the earth and ultimately into the world's food chain. Every time that you clean you are helping pollute the planet.

Are the personal care products – the toothpaste, the shampoo, the soap, the deodorant, etc - you use on your body, also chemically based? Then they are counter-productive to your good health. Your skin can absorb traces of these often harsh and poisonous chemicals and your body may not be able to respond by eliminating them.

If you answered yes to any of the above then it is time to consider changing to environmentally friendly ones. The products might not currently be available in your local mainstream supermarket but begin there, as their management is sensitive to what their customers want, so the more of us who ask for these products the more likely we will be able to make change happen – and make a difference to not only our own health, but the health of the planet. The internet hosts many retailers who will deliver a multitude of eco-friendly products to you quickly, economically and most probably in recycled packaging.

♥ My Action Plan

- ❏ I eat natural unprocessed foods as often as I am able, including something that I have grown

- ❏ I embrace knowing that I am Source and acknowledge that anything I do to abuse my body can lead to imperfect health

- ❏ I embrace the complementary properties of non-mainstream medicines and therapies and I am open to their benefits

- ❏ Aromatherapy adds benefits throughout my day and throughout my life

- ❏ I embrace spending time in the natural world

- ❏ I take positive action towards my perfect health especially by choosing eco-friendly cleaning products and natural personal care products

CHAPTER NINE

LIVING THE NEW EARTH PHILOSOPHY

"The most valuable things in life are not measured in monetary terms. The really important things are not houses and lands, stock and bonds, automobiles and real estate, but friendships, trust, confidence, empathy, mercy, love and faith."

- Bertrand Russell
British Philosopher 1872-1970

Living A Purer, Happier And More Harmonious Life

In this chapter we will take a look at those things in our life, or that we can attract in to our life, that can bring renewed happiness and contentment, joyousness and harmony.

None of them are earth shattering or expensive, but they have been around in one form or another for a very long time. Perhaps we have simply lost contact with them over the years and we just need a small reminder to help us realign our spirit with them.

Share Your Life With A Pet

Our pets, especially cats and dogs, can help ground us to love. They rely on us for their life needs of food, water and health care. In return they give us unconditional love and we instinctively know that not only must we return it but that we want to. As we play with them, pat them, attend to their needs we can see nothing but loyalty and love in their eyes. They adore us for who we are, and make no judgments about our gender, race, skin color, age, religious beliefs, culture or financial standing. The relationship between pet and 'owner' is a microcosm of the unconditional love that Source is to our selves. Each is as one with the other.

Why do I advocate an animal as part of your life?

1) Focus and Companionship – you are their provider and therefore you have responsibility, an obligation, a focus, to feed, groom, protect and care for them. Like a helpless human baby they are totally reliant on you. By sharing your life with them you are actively

thinking and helping create a loving world where all humans and creatures harmoniously co-exist

2) Unconditual Love – they live a pure spiritual life, and so should we. Live to share with others, give of your love freely and generously, ask nothing of others but love in return. Expect to be fed and sheltered because of the love you share. Our animals only have love and companionship to give, and this they give – unconditionally

3) Happiness - the sheer joy they give you. Everyone who is sharing unconditional love with an animal is already a practicing New Age student. You *know* what it feels like to be unconditionally loved, you *know* of the loving bonds that already exist between living entities and as a result, you *know* the harmony and joyous energy that abounds within you.

So today set aside time to spend with your animal companion simply being adoring friends with each other. Play, romp, tickle, pat, laugh, share secrets, look into each other's eyes – and above all, feel the love and feel the happiness. And notice how it comes back to you in abundance.

Your life is guaranteed to change for the better.

Find Good In Everything

> *"Wherever there is a human being,*
> *there is an opportunity for a kindness."*
>
> - Seneca
> Roman Philosopher 4BC–65AD

A loving heart always finds the good seed even in the most rotten of apples.

Don't be overwhelmed by the aggressive, the cold exterior or the brutal outside image of another human. It's often hiding something very tender and painful deep inside. Even if we don't know what pains they carry, we can send them healing love. Whatever the exterior, love can penetrate that barrier. The vibrations of love can find their way into the most intricate of cavities, can penetrate the toughest materials and can travel unimpeded to the ends of the known world. Know this, and don't be put off by physical impressions. Understand that love freely given, carries with it the highest of pure vibrations. It carries enlightenment, healing, creativity – all the keys to unlocking the frigidity, frailty and pain of the human heart.

Of course, love can be rejected by the exercise of free will by the recipient. Not everyone can or will accept our unconditional love but that should not stop us from sending it.

You may never know or understand whether your unconditional love was received, acted upon or used for healing. But do know that it raised the vibrations of the spiritual world by at least another notch. It might be the equivalent of a mere raindrop but when added to by other "raindrops of love" then a stream happens, and then they form to become a sea of love. Any love sent from the heart is never lost, never wasted. It remains circling and purifying the earth and lifting the vibrations for all.

Never miss an opportunity to send love or show kindness. As the preceding quote from Seneca indicates even the Romans understood its importance and in today's global madness it is even more relevant.

At this moment can you honestly say that the earth is a better and more loving place because you have lived here?

Bring Stillness In To Your Life

Stillness allows me to detach from the world circulating around me. I am the calm nucleus in a swirling sea of activity. I observe but I am not of that tempestuous world.

My stillness comes about through observation. As I go about my day I focus on objects and people, and as I do, I see texture.

Do you have a favorite tree? Then embrace it, touch the trunk, feel the bark, smell the blossoms, admire the leafy canopy, give gratitude for all the benefits it brings to you, the birds, the insects, the moss, the bees, the animals it shelters and the oxygen it produces for us to breathe.

I observe the wonder of a tree that grew from a tiny seed. I see the rivulets of aging on the protective bark. I see the intricate veins within the fragility of the leaf. I imagine the rivers of sap and moisture being its lifelines. I see a bird's nest, a marching army of ants or a spider waiting for a catch in its web.

The result is that I have stopped my treadmill of life activities for a few minutes. By focusing on the tree I have left the everyday world and temporarily moved into a new reality – my tree. It's as if I have drilled down into a new layer of reality. Instead of always just quickly observing 'the big picture' I'm now looking at the detail – and that detail is astonishing.

I become totally as one with the tree: the outside 'real' world is still there but it is lost to me. My stillness comes from connecting with nature, with a living wonder that exists without my help. It seeded, grew, blossomed, and exists as part of the natural world. I too am of the natural world, of the same Source as is the tree and all it's inhabitants.

For those few moments where the tree and I are one, there is a quiet connection to the natural rhythms of the earth – a rhythm that we tend to forget, or ignore or are too busy to discover. My heart and my soul embrace these moments and truly understand that we are all connected and live here as one.

In my quietness, I also return to me – that deep recess where there is stillness, a place of quiet reflection and the spring from whence my love derives. In these moments I can renew my conscious connection to it and drink amply from its energy and purity.

This is but one example of calming the soul. You will discover others that you can relate to.

Consider

- Reclining on grass and getting lost in the patterns of the clouds
- Walking solo in large public gardens
- Picking fruit at a berry farm
- Hiking forest trails with a social walking group
- Volunteering at an animal shelter
- Assisting in restoring a garden, getting your hands into the soil

- Cooking a special surprise meal for your elderly neighbor

- Sitting in a church in quiet contemplation

- Building and maintaining a bird table

The important thing is that you do find ways of removing yourself from the everyday hustle of this world and find inner quietness. It is very restorative.

Thank Your Unseen Support Staff

We don't travel this earth-plane alone. We all have our unseen guides, healers, angels, loved ones and teachers working with us and supporting us from other dimensions.

Constantly talk to them. Ask their advice. Share your joy with them. Treat them as you best friends. Know that they are your divine connection to dimensions and worlds we can't begin to imagine. Their conduit to you will bring you everything you can imagine. They love you and want you to succeed in whatever your heart desires. That's their purpose of being with you. You're a team.

So take time throughout your day to silently say "Thank you" to them. Express your gratitude - and look and listen for the answers to the questions you've asked, observe your world for the strategically-placed clues in regards to your life journey and when courage is required, know that you are *never* alone. Above all, continue your joyous life knowing that you are blessed, loved and protected - *always!*

Let Your Inner Child Have Fun

Sometime in our eagerness to learn New Age techniques and philosophies we can become too earnest in our endeavors.

We focus on discovering books and articles, attending New Age fairs and lectures and learning about whatever we can that resonates with us. Then with enthusiasm and energy we put these newly learned activities into practice – and sometimes to the detriment of having fun.

New Age/New Earth is about joy and loving our life and embracing whom that we are. Sometimes we need reminding that our inner child has to be looked after too. That wide-eyed, non-materialistic, free-playing and joyous child who still lives deep within us requires attention – and play time.

Today, make a pact with your inner child that, at least for a period each and every day from now on, you will live joyously and with abandon, free from what others might expect of you as an adult.

Take your shoes off and paddle in the ocean, fold up your umbrella and feel what rain really is like as it hits your skin, eat dessert before you have a main meal, watch DVDs all night and sleep all day, go fly a kite, write and send a poem to someone you admire, drop a note in a bottle and set it adrift on the sea, spend the day at home totally nude.

These are all things that don't cost money; they are us taking control of our beautiful day; they are us living a freedom and joyousness that nourishes our soul, liberates our consciousness and tunes us into the love and joy that permeates our world. Through laughter and spontaneity we are abandoning control over our thinking and therefore living as close to our true inner being as possible.

When you do hear that inner giggle of childhood laughter you know that today has been the best ever. You will have freed yourself from the confines of a dull, beige-colored and constricted existence and embraced true happiness.

Spontaneous Dancing

I particularly enjoy being me, the individual, when there's no obligation or desire to be anywhere else or with any one else.

Perhaps I've been writing, listening to the music on the radio whilst I cook or I've just returned home from some happy experience - and I am filled with a restless energy. Those are times when I want to express myself by merging completely into the imagery of my mind or connecting to the pulse of the music I adore.

It's then that I have a spontaneous free-movement moment and simply let my body respond to the vibrations. I sing, or swirl about, or dance or close my eyes and move sublimely in a meditative world, being as one with the universe.

It may be a fleeting moment or it may last for many minutes. Either way it is a release from the every day world and acts as a glorious example of the potential I have within me to move further into universal oneness.

Imagine that walking-on-air feeling after a massage, that meditative feeling when having your hair cut or brushed, the alertness when waking from a power-nap and you will have some idea of not only the feeling of release from your everyday routine but glimpse how delightful merging with other dimensions can be. It's liberating and highly recommended.

And perhaps we really don't have to worry about who is watching – they're probably pre-occupied reading their latest social media message on their phone or tablet and paying no attention to us at all!

Living With The Abundance Of Life

Taking an insect from your home and letting it fly free in the open air in my view epitomizes the Buddhist approach to life, of live and let live, of every creature being part of the Cycle of Life.

I'm not perfect in this regard (with spiders, mosquitoes and flies still at my mercy), but I am getting better at gently collecting the insect from the inside of my window and carefully relocating it to the outside world. My 3D approach of "how dare this insect invade my private territory and annoy me" is being replaced with the 4D knowledge that it and I are as one.

Rather than kill, I relocate – that satisfies my own spatial demands and allows the insect freedom to be itself. For me, all it took was a little bit of effort to actually capture, transport and release it unharmed.

The first time I did this was a significant moment…

Firstly, because it was an action so out of the ordinary for me that it registered a 'why am I doing this' moment of reflection - me the huge human comparing myself to the insect so small and delicate. Was this something about being fatherly and thus caring for the small members of the family, or was it a chink in my armor where the 'thou shall not kill' commandment still quietly exists to remind me of my spirituality?

Secondly, it felt good. I had not let my ego interfere in the natural rhythms of the earth-plane life cycle. Now on different paths, both the insect and I could continue with our natural life progression. We both exist for a purpose and in my act of allowing 'live and let live' I tapped into a deep inner reservoir of love, respect and wisdom. It was a wake-up call to respect all life wherever I would come upon it. Human, animal, insect, plant, fish or bird we are all connected and part of the majesty of the natural world.

And you know what – it gets easier to share your life with the insect population, so much so that relocation is now getting rarer. I see the insect within my home, I share a moment of mutual admiration and thanks, I give it the respect for what it is, I send it love – and we silently agree to continue our day doing our own thing in our own way – inside the house – together!

As we are both creatures of Source my day then remains peaceful, calm and joyful as we each continue to live our own life path.

Admire The Delicate Petals Of A Flower

I endeavor to find a moment or two in each day to admire Nature's amazing diversity and handiwork. And looking closely into a flower head says it all for me.

"You are closest to God's heart in a garden" is another saying that my wise mother frequently shared with me. Whatever word you use for God, the truth within these words

remains the same – you are as one with the Creator, with Source.

Admire the delicacy and the designs of the petals, the color, the intricate mechanisms of the stamens, the pollen. No human has as yet designed or created such a beautiful, functional and delicate body.

The extraordinary intricate designs, colors, sizes, shapes, mechanisms and purpose of all living creatures could only have been created by a powerful energy source beyond any concept my brain can imagine. I am in awe of such energy but equally I know that I am already part of it.

Frequently Give Thanks

Frequently say "Thank you" - anytime, anywhere - for the life-giving beauty and energy of which you are part. Think it, whisper it, shout it or write it – whatever way you express it your gratitude will be enmeshed into the living web of interconnectedness. As you now know, we are pure Source energy, so anything we say or do or think moves from us into that energy web, and like a mirror, reflects back to us what we give out – multiplied!

Your "Thank you" is never lost in the ether.

Give thanks for the physical blessings in your life – a roof over your head, clothing, electricity, running hot and cold water, money (no matter how much or how little), your physical body, your senses (sight, hearing, touch, your voice), the car, the furniture, your loving cat or dog, the computer, cutlery, growing your own vegetables and fruits, a comfortable bed. The list is seemingly endless. Basically any and everything you possess, touch, use or share brings a blessing in to your life. Give gratitude for it having been attracted to you for your use.

You should also acknowledge the intangible abilities and gifts associated with your individual life - your worldly knowledge and accumulated wisdom, your health, your ability to read, to change your viewpoint, your instincts, singing ability, your love for family, friends and people you haven't met yet – and I'm sure you can think of many, many more.

In your life – wherever and whoever you are – you cannot express too much gratitude.

Gratitude expressed through a loving heart is the very essence of a joyous existence!

Celebrate Every Day

Why can't every day be filled with ordinary joys? It can! And it's already happening. I observe the good cheer, the tolerance, the caring comments given to neighbors and strangers, the smile and good wishes shared across a retail counter, the softness of the heart when observing wide-eyed children as they are indulged, the self-sacrificing effort and the many miles traveled by some people to be with loved ones.

There is a joy in the air; there is love in action.

So let's say hello to our elderly neighbor as she tends her garden, encourage the child sitting opposite you on the bus to laugh, give some non-perishable food to your local social service community, prepare an unexpected celebratory meal for your family, book a vacation visit to see distant relatives, give of your time to a worthy volunteer organization, visit a religious building and listen to the music or sit silently in meditative gratitude for your abundant life.

When all of us decide to take the time each day to celebrate the joy of life on this beautiful earth and to share time to care for one another, then what a wonderful legacy we will give to our children and our children's children.

Be a loving and committed example of where this shared love begins.

Adjust Your Self-Image

We all carry them – the image(s) that we *perceive* ourselves to look like to other people. Most likely there are different images for different people. In every case they are the result of our imaginings and experiences.

To live up to them takes a good deal of effort and adjustment. There's the balancing act between the different images. You may be a mother to someone, a sister to another, a teacher to someone else, a concerned activist to another, a devoted pet owner to someone else.

The images may also be negative – I'm over-weight and therefore unattractive. My cultural background scares potential lovers. I'll be judged by the way I maintain my home. My grey hair makes me look older than I am. My lack of education makes me unsuitable. I'm not confidant enough to be a good volunteer.

These are all judgments that you have made about yourself. Were you once hurt by someone's scathing remarks and you don't ever want that feeling again? Does television keep reinforcing stereotypes that imply that you would be unsuitable to fit in to that way of life? You've observed that someone close to you basks in the glory of appreciative comments about being a fine cook yet your cooking you label as perfunctory.

It's time to decide to change this thinking. Your self-image is, I repeat, *perceived.* You are trying to be someone else. To be everything to everyone – and you can't be. You can only be true to yourself.

You now know that you are the purity of Source itself. You are a special, unique individual, warts and all. We all have 'warts' of some kind, whether they be physical, emotional, cultural or spiritual.

They are the things that make us so special, different, unique. We know and appreciate that they are part of us, but they don't need to stop us achieving being ourselves.

We do ourselves a great disservice by under valuing who we really are. Yes, some avenues of growth may be closed to us because of a wart/disability, but there are other ways to work towards happiness where the wart will not stop us. Those with a physical disability only have to look to the Para Olympic Games participants for inspiration. People with dyslexia achieve outstanding educational and business management results. How those who have to give a eulogy at a funeral find courage and realize they can do public speaking and do it very successfully under trying circumstances.

How we value ourselves is a reflection of how we perceive what others expect of us. It's time to stop guessing what they might think and time to say "this is what I've been dealt in life physically, educationally and emotionally so from this day on I'm going to use what I have, be proud and at ease with myself and start utilizing those under-developed areas of my life." When we begin to grasp the potentials that this earth-plane life offers us then that is when we become closer to Source.

Just Be Yourself

Live your life filled with energy and compassion.

Share your time and your wisdom for you don't always know how it influences others. Many times we do good deeds simply by living our life without realizing the enormous influence we can have on those we share it with.

In my own life I have been blessed with comments from people who have confided to me months or even years later, that I was the "right person at the right time".

In most instances I saw it simply as sharing my time, offering a shoulder to lean on, perhaps implanting a little wisdom, being a friend. But when someone tells you that talking out their crisis issue with you saved him or her from taking their own life, you realize that just being you can make a huge difference.

If you are optimistic, loving, willing to share time, show calmness, be grateful - then you can give others hope, clarity and an example to strive for. Not all your examples will be as dramatic as my one, but recall now how you felt when someone you helped presented you with a flower to symbolize their gratitude. Didn't it feel fantastic to be acknowledged with love?

Today, just by giving a smile and a cheery "hello" you can bring love and happiness to another soul. You may be the only one to do so that day. In particular, cities can be both crowded yet very lonely places. A ray of love sent unconditionally to a fellow human is the greatest gift you can give. And monetarily, it doesn't cost anything.

Smile, give out love and live this beautiful life that you are truly destined to enjoy.

Positive Mental Attitude

A positive mental attitude is also highly beneficial for a smooth and abundant life.

By believing in, and living within Source, you are at the Divine Heart of the universe. Don't think that Source might work 93% of the time, or I'll have some form of lifestyle bet on the side just to cover myself. No – Source *is* perfection, it is energy, it is the core for connecting the entire web of atoms and molecules in the universe. Maintaining a positive mental attitude means that you have total belief that you are indeed as one with Source.

In my old 3D world I finally realized that I spent too much time with negatively minded people. Today when I encounter them I bless them, and then move to an area of my world where I am not listening to their draining and destructive approach to life.

I know that I am a positive energy that drives my life in happy and loving and thankful directions. I no longer join in the collective destructive voice that opposes another's point of view or action. Have you noticed that the loudest and most energized voices are often the most negative ones?

Change happens through love and harmony, and through the interconnected web of togetherness. I don't have to confront the negative antagonist – I simply withdraw and send my love and harmony silently to them.

Change happens when enough of us do the same!

Even though there may be many issues to overcome on your journey, possibly including depression, anxiety, fear, or more, you are traveling with the one and only power that combines us all, so you now know that everything is possible. With such powerful alignment in your life, who wouldn't maintain a totally positive attitude to the future?

Be Outgoing And Friendly

Always be outgoing and friendly, and enjoy your life by sharing the company of other positive and spiritual souls.

I learn a great deal about the world and myself when I share conversation with strangers. My genuine appearance of friendliness attracts people to me. And it is the least obvious person who will often provide the greatest insights for me. Many times they also give me the answer to a question that I have placed in the hands of the universe. They don't know that, but in my own mind I have a "wow" moment where answers effortlessly click together and connect.

This also connects to synchronicity. I can receive silent indicators about subject matters I should endeavor to follow up and learn more about. Perhaps I receive an idea for my writing or a warning not to proceed in a particular direction. I am constantly learning from the people I 'accidentally' meet (and as you very well know, there are no 'accidental' meetings, only learning opportunities). So, be outgoing, friendly, loving – and always with an open mind.

Promise yourself that today you will chat with that person waiting with you at the bus stop, share a table in a crowded coffee shop or talk to the person sitting next to you at the theatre. I guarantee that your heart will be a little lighter, your outlook a little more expanded and there will be an inner satisfaction because of the connection. By sharing a caring moment or two you might also learn how fortunate you really are. Whatever connection we make, we benefit from it.

Enjoy Your Abundance

By embracing the New Earth we aren't looking to become hermits, totally detached from the every day world but rather we embrace new possibilities, receiving gifts that invoke our imagination, help us communicate, lift our vibrations or encourage us to create and learn.

It seems to me that the universe has a master plan for humanity that includes peaceful co-existence with one another, shared harmonious joy, spiritual education and positive upliftment. When we combine our desires for physical items and they come in to our lives, then we should use them for these ends. Let's communicate via computers, the internet and cell phones. Let's read about new aspects of spirituality on our tablets. Download music from clouds, drive our cars, make and share videos, watch inspiring movies and documentaries, conveniently carry music with us wherever we go and indulge in good food with the money we attract.

Hobbies bring us joy both as individuals and when shared with others. Use that sewing machine, art easel or tool set to create or repair. Be aware of your creative intelligence whilst enjoying your hobby and then share the result either by gifting the item or displaying it for the inspiration of others.

Perhaps it's also time to rediscover those souvenir items you purchased on vacation many years ago. Admire them, and recall the discovery and purchase moment. Select some of them for display and revel in the happy memories they engender. That can be a rock from a particular beach, a toy soldier from an ancient castle, a nice T-shirt from an historic site or a photo of the tour group.

They are great reminders of happy times, but they are also reminders of our abundance. We have desired and received money to pay for the travel, to buy the cell phone, to take hobby classes - there is already a history of abundance in your life, a proven track record.

When you desire man-made products that will enhance your spiritual life through their ability to support your 4D thinking, this is a good thing. Just remember that need is not the same as desire. Keep your affirmations within the *desire* area and you will attract the abundance you want.

In the meantime, enjoy the spiritual happiness that the items you already have are giving you and say "Thank you" for the great abundance that is already in your life.

As we look forward to tomorrow, it's the "Thank you" for yesterday we can too easily overlook.

Continue Using, Don't Unnecessarily Replace

We've all been seemingly brainwashed into thinking obsolescence is a good thing.

Instinctively we know that as a population we are devastating the planet through our collective demand for 'new', 'better' or 'improved' products. I'm not against an improved lifestyle, but I deplore planned obsolescence in the name of financial profits and harm to our planet.

I grew up in a post-war world of shortage, austerity and personal sacrifice for my parents, and this has colored my view of the world ever since. Perhaps you grew up later, in a time of more abundance and a staggering range of products. Now as an adult of this latter era, yours is a time where the popular creed is to chase abundant money, buy the latest product or fashion accessory and to live in a grossly material world.

As baby boomers we've been there too. As we've aged and become more affluent, we've also indulged in the pleasures of available products.

But surprisingly, as I have aged, I've discovered that I need less new gadgets, less trinkets cluttering the shelves, only one or two of something and not the multiple of a item that can sit unused in cupboards. If an item does what I want it to why upgrade to something new just because of a few more bells and whistles that I probably wouldn't use?

My cell/mobile phone is truly ancient – but it does what I want of it. It receives calls, I can call out, I can text a message, I can see the current time, it holds a few addresses, the screen is small and in black and white, and there is no internet access. No one would ever steal it, it bounces when it's dropped and it's a bit bulky. But it works!

Sure, I'll upgrade sometime, but probably only to another hand-me-down device that is no longer of use to another person. Why send it to landfill. I'm happy to keep using products if they work. I'm going to do my bit to help stop the atrocious waste of the earth's resources by removing my need to acquire just because of color, model or some other minor change.

Acquisition for its own sake is not 4D living. Happiness with what you already have around you is a great beginning to peace and contentment in your life. Certainly add items to your vision board and your law of attraction desire list, but make them useful to you, and in the size that is practical. We don't need abundance just for the sake of owning; we need to cut our cloth to that which we can comfortably enjoy.

If all of us in the abundant, materially-possessed, affluent areas of the world only bought and used what we actually needed to live comfortably - and changed our shopping habits to tell the manufactures that we don't want such an over-abundance – I suspect our world would be a better place.

Spiritually we would see that what we have in our everyday lives is more than enough, and through gratitude we would have the peaceful mind to enjoy it.

Laugh At Yourself

We can take ourselves far too seriously. Genuine laughter is a wonderful form of relief – both emotional and physical.

It's as close to joy as many allow themselves to come. Get used to laughter, and joy will soon also share your life. Don't laugh to be spiteful or hurtful to others. But laugh to see that sometimes we humans become a little too entrenched in our beliefs and that there is another way of looking at that lifestyle. Though laughter is a very personal thing where some will laugh whilst others will sit stony-faced, today try to find the lighter side of life. Give yourself permission to smile inside your soul, or to laugh out loud. Lift the vibrations of the earth with your droplet of laughter and happiness.

Smile

Nothing communicates better than a warm smile. Whether you need to diffuse an aggressive situation, encourage another to be more positive or you meet a stranger who asks you for directions - give out your smile.

A smile is a reflection of your inner being. It states to the outside world that you are filled with joy and earth energy;

that you are not being aggressive; that you give out love. And the medical experts tell us that it takes less effort to smile than frown!

Give of that wonderful smile of yours to everyone you meet today. Feel how easy it is to do, and see and feel the resulting free-flow of love returned to you.

A smile warms every heart it beams upon.

> *"We shall never know all the good that a simple smile can do."*
>
> - Mother Teresa
> Catholic Sister, Missionary 1910-1997

Share Kindness

No one was ever harmed by too much kindness!

As part of your gratitude in action, give to others all manner of kindness. Give your unconditional love, give kind words, your caring, your encouragement and your support in whatever ways seem suitable.

Kindness is about supporting others during their times of difficulty. Whatever the circumstances, your shared empathy can make a difference. Even a single word or simply being there, can turn the tide toward them feeling wanted, loved, nurtured. Remember that the more love we give the more that returns to us. Invest in kindness for a guaranteed profitable return in your life.

Don't let a day go by (or even an hour) without a show of kindness. Giving and gratitude are two of the most powerful factors we have in our personal arsenal as we head towards a peaceful, calm and abundant life journey.

♥ *My Action Plan*

- ❏ I actively seek happiness and harmony in my daily life through such actions as sharing with pets and finding good in everyone and everything

- ❏ I reserve a small part of my day to listen to the stillness

- ❏ I frequently acknowledge throughout the day my unseen guides, healers, angels and other loved ones

- ❏ I love to laugh, dance, take time with nature, celebrate my abundance and be eternally grateful for everything that is in my life

- ❏ I love being me

- ❏ I associate only with positive, like-minded people and enjoy sharing friendship moments with strangers

- ❏ I believe in myself and appreciate my partnership with Source

- ❏ I carefully consider my purchasing practices and do not replace items unnecessarily

- ❏ Throughout my day I laugh, smile and share kindness with others

CHAPTER TEN

YOU ARE...

"I am, just as you are, a unique, never-to-be-repeated event in this universe. Therefore, I have, just as you have, a unique, never-to-be-repeated role in this world."

- George Sheehan
Cardiologist, Runner, Writer 1918-1993

No One Else Sees The World Like You Do

– So don't fight their view or try to convert them. They have a right to their own views and to express those views. Appreciate that their experiences have lead them to a different conclusion from yours.

Whether you feel that their views are right or wrong for them, appreciate that their views will be different from yours in small or large ways. Whether they are happy or unhappy with their situation is entirely their journey. You're not going to judge them based on your opinion, as this would be succumbing to your ego. You are free to follow your own spiritual or religious path and so are they.

Our role is to live our life in the happiest way that *we* can, filled with love and joy and gratitude. By living this life perhaps others will notice and seek aspects of value that will change or enhance their own beliefs. We must never allow ourselves to be a dictating spiritual force.

Let us beam out our joys and be happy with that. If others see us in this natural, happy state then we are a walking example worthy of emulation. When asked for our secret then we can share our philosophy and methodology.

Live For Today

Live today filled with energy, joy and happiness. Embrace all of the possibilities and indulge in the ones that best suit your temperament.

Share your day with like-minded souls, touch the earth's natural state, let your spirit fly to higher lightness, be as one with the flow of the life-stream.

Yesterday is memory, history that can't be changed; it is indelibly carved into your past. It is behind you and you no longer dwell there.

Tomorrow will probably shine brightly, but that's not certain.

Just yesterday a friend telephoned to say that his brother had a severe stroke a month ago. My friend has now given up his job to become his brother's full-time caregiver. In an instant two lives changed. No doubt you also know of similar life-altering moments.

Today is right now, this instant. Speaking personally, I don't want to be anywhere else. Through me flows everything that ever was; is right now; and can be. I am connected to everyone and everything. All I need to do is to activate the inner switch and through love let anything I desire connect to me. That's equivalent to a billion lotto wins and it's all freely there for my asking.

Don't let another moment go by without focusing on what you want - and then live to the maximum whilst it prepares to come to you.

Your Legacy

As you grow older it's natural to begin to ask the question about whether you have done enough to leave a lasting legacy.

I'm not talking about world shattering ideas and actions here, but I am talking about a minimum of one heart or mind (and hopefully many more) that would miss your presence. In other words, I'm talking about a heart (or a mind) that has been positively influenced by your love, your forgiveness and/or your gratitude.

Take a moment to reflect on who would be likely to attend your funeral service. And would these people be in some way correlated to the love that you currently spread through your actions?

We have all been given talents that we can recognize as helpful to humanity. To act on them and bring their potential benefits to our fellow man and woman is our role in life.

I believe that I'm part of something indefinably larger that needs my specific talents and energies. If I fail to use these gifts then others are let down by my inertia and in a small way the earth is deprived of yet another positive action for change and betterment.

Today, anything that you do for another person is using your special gifts and this is an action that will mirror itself back to you and you will receive back in abundance. Any loving action - no matter the size - places an essence of your love into another's heart that will stay there for eternity.

What a joy this world would be to live in if all humanity gave unconditional love back to every person they met every day. We can do our part - and isn't that a stunning legacy for all of us to leave behind!

Your Every Day Reality Mirrors Who You Really Are

Mirrors reflect what they see; scenery, people, rooms, it doesn't matter.

Mirrors don't change anything unless they are in some way manufactured to purposely distort.

Think of the universe as a mirror. Whatever you give out – your physical body image, love, joy, anger, fear – it bounces back, exactly as you gave it out. And what you gave out is also exactly what others see when they look at you.

A mirror doesn't hide anything, enhance anything or pretend that something is not as it is.

Based on your current belief system is there something you see that isn't right, something that pricks your conscious? Something that is telling you that change is required?

If you are giving out anger then why does it seem that situations that make you angry are lined up facing you? If you are giving out a poverty mentality why is it that nothing like money comes your way to alleviate your situation? If you give out envy why is it that the winners are always someone other than you? Whatever surrounds you, good or bad, abundant or scarce, has been attracted to you by your beliefs.

In short, what you are giving out to the universe is connecting to like matter.

As there is no way that you can change such natural laws it's *you* and *your attitude* that has to change. Live with your dissatisfaction - or decide this very minute, that you need to change.

Having read this book and others like it, I suspect that you have already realized that change is essential if you want to improve the level of joy and abundance in your life. It's *your* choice. Now it's entirely up to *you*!

I Am Unique. You Are Unique

This book has offered nothing new that hasn't been spoken or written about somewhere in the world over the many centuries where beliefs have been documented.

What I have offered is a unique combination of beliefs, philosophies and practices that have proven *right for me*. It's the first time in the whole history of mankind that it has happened, and what this overview gives you is the opportunity to write your own belief sheet, one that will allow *you* to soar in a manner that feels totally comfortable. This comfort is your inner instinct, your all-knowing soul telling you that at last you have arrived 'Home' and that from now on life *will* be what you want.

In the whole history of mankind there's never been another combination like yours – you're unique.

So choose what suits you from these guidelines and laws that have been given to us from thinkers, scribes, philosophers, manifest Masters, visionaries, mystics, shaman, and many others. We have every piece of knowledge that we need to make our own lives unique, comfortable, abundant, healthy and peaceful.

Begin the dance to your own special piece of music. Make a commitment right now that you *can* – and you *will* – become as one with the entire universe. That your music will not be lost to the noise and hubbub of everyday survival and even though you are the only one hearing the melody right now, in due course yours will be a chorus that will be shared by the good-willed, like-minded hearts of this world.

Live in joy, dance with abandon, smile like sunshine, thank your particular God Source, embrace peace and send unconditional love to infiltrate every heart.

When that happens you will indeed be 'Home'.

Enjoy your abundant, happy and wonderful new 4D life! May the rest of your life be the best of your life.

*"Go confidently in the direction of your dreams.
Live the life you have imagined."*

Henry David Thoreau
American Author, Poet, Philosopher 1817-1862

www.peterbenn.com

www.ingramcontent.com/pod-product-compliance
Lightning Source LLC
Chambersburg PA
CBHW050634300426
44112CB00012B/1794